CONTENTS

THE RISE AND FALL OF THE SOVIET EMPIRE

THE RISE AND FALL OF THE S★VIET EMPIRE

STEPHEN DALZIEL

SMITHMARK

This edition published in 1993
by SMITHMARK Publishers Inc.,
16 East 32nd Street
New York, New York 10016.

SMITHMARK books are available for bulk purchase
for sales promotion and premium use. For details
write or telephone the Manager of Special Sales,
SMITHMARK Publishers Inc., 16 East 32nd Street,
New York, NY 10016. (212) 532-6600.

Produced by Brompton Books Corp.,
15 Sherwood Place,
Greenwich, CT 06830.

ISBN 0-8317-7368-5

Printed in Hong Kong

10 9 8 7 6 5 4 3 2 1

The author would like to thank friends and colleagues
at the BBC World Service who helped with proof-reading,
comments and suggestions in the writing of this
book. Special thanks are due to Malcolm Haslett,
Rob Parsons, Gabriel Partos and Jan Repa. Any
errors which remain, and all opinions expressed,
are the author's own.
Stephen Dalziel
January 1993

PAGES 2-3: A statue of Lenin, leader of the
Russian Revolution and founder of the Soviet
state, in Novosibirsk, Siberia.

1
THE
LEGACY OF CZARISM

'The empire is dead. Long live the empire!' No Bolshevik who took part in the Russian Revolution of November 1917 would have dared to suggest that their seizure of power meant just that. The very idea of 'an empire,' wherein a powerful center controlled and exploited colonies it had conquered was complete anathema to Karl Marx and Vladimir Lenin, the founding fathers of Communism. Indeed, in one of his principal works in the years leading up to the Revolution, Lenin had described imperialism as, 'the highest stage of capitalism.' The idea of a Communist empire was supposed to be a contradiction in terms.

Yet in practice, Soviet Russia came to represent not one but three empires. The first it inherited from its predecessors, the czars. The second it created by its own conquests after World War II. The third was an ideological empire worldwide which had mixed success. Ironically, this attempt to spread Soviet influence by means of an imperialistic foreign policy saw a reversal of the idea that the center of the empire exploited the colonies. The Soviet Union actually weakened itself by spending billions trying to spread the revolution.

The first empire – that established on the territory of the Soviet Union itself – owed much to the 1000 or so years of history which preceded it. It also contained within it a number of the seeds of its own disintegration which were to flourish only in the latter part of the 1980s. The country which the Bolsheviks took over in 1917 was already by far the largest in the world. It had begun as the state of Rus' in the late ninth century and through a series of wars and peaceful exploration had grown into a sprawling mass encompassing everything from the middle of Europe to the Pacific Ocean.

Kiev was the first capital of a Russian state, and has always been known as 'the mother of Russian cities.' A consequence of the break-up of the Soviet Union in 1991 was that Russia became an orphan, its 'mother' being the capital of the newly-independent Ukraine. Early Russian history was more about internal feuding than serious attempts to construct a nation-state, let alone an empire. The first unifying factor was imposed from without, when the Mongol hordes invaded and captured much of the Russian lands from the twelfth century onward. It took 300 years before there was anything like a united attempt to throw off 'the Mongol yoke' and extend Russia's boundaries into the lands occupied by its former oppressors.

It was under Ivan IV (often known as Ivan the Terrible) that Russian expansion began in earnest. He took advantage of internal divisions

BELOW: Lenin addressing Bolshevik troops in Red Square, Moscow, 1919.

among the Mongols to seize Kazan in 1552 and Astrakhan three years later. Not only did this give Russia control over the entire length of the River Volga, but it also paved the way to more peaceful expansion into Siberia over the next 300 years. The dominant powers to the west of Russia were Poland, Livonia and Sweden. From the second half of the sixteenth century until the end of the eighteenth, Russia was almost continuously at war with these neighbors. The most notable victory in this period was achieved by Peter the Great over Sweden. When the Great Northern War was concluded by the Peace of Nystad in 1721, after 21 years of fighting, Russia gained possession of Livonia, Estonia, Ingria and Karelia, and was established as the dominant power in northwestern Europe. To celebrate the peace, the Senate and the Holy Synod confered on Peter the title of 'emperor,' signifying the end of the state of Muscovy and the start of the Russian empire.

The next major expansion of the empire took place under the Empress Catherine II (1762-1796). As well as expanding Russia's territory in northwestern Europe, Catherine waged wars against Turkey and Persia. From Turkey, Russia gained the port of Azov (on the Sea of Azov) and much of the Black Sea coast in what is now Ukraine. This included the Crimean peninsula, which was to become an object of great controversy after the break-up of the Soviet Union. Never a part of Ukraine, it was given to that republic by the then Soviet leader Nikita Khrushchev in 1954 as a gift to mark 300 years of union between Russia and Ukraine. When Ukraine became independent, many Russians began to question the legality of Khrushchev's action.

Victory over Persia in 1796 extended Russian influence into Transcaucasia. This was the start of the incorporation of modern-day Georgia, Armenia and Azerbaijan into the empire, something which was achieved in stages throughout the nineteenth century. Farther east, the nineteenth century also saw the incorporation of Central Asia into the Russian empire. This was carried out largely peacefully, especially in the 1860s and 1870s. The rest of Siberia was also conquered, and territories were acquired on the borders with China and Mongolia by the Far Eastern Treaties of 1858 and 1860. Russia even occupied Alaska, but sold it to America in 1867.

One feature of Russian expansion in the nineteenth century was to lead to discontent in the empire. This was the policy of 'Russification.' Non-Russian communities were persecuted, heavy taxes imposed and local languages banned. This was one reason why some parts of the empire sought and achieved independence

BELOW: An early engraving of the city of Kazan. Ivan the Terrible drove the Tatars out of Kazan in 1552. It is now the capital of Tatarstan, a republic pressing for independence from Russia.

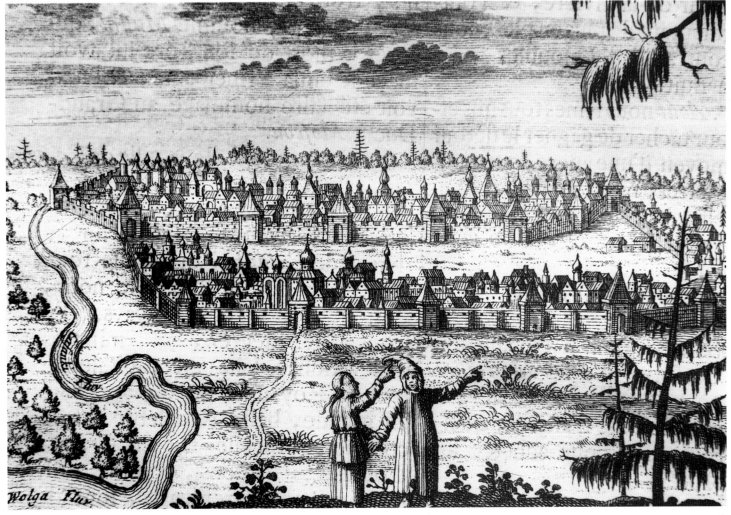

after World War I, but it also served as a model for Soviet rulers in the years to come and was to lead to great discontent which erupted when the Communist system collapsed at the end of the 1980s.

Another model which the Soviet leaders took from their Russian predecessors was that of 'the firm fist' in government. No other country has such a history of cruel and despotic leaders. The example set in particular by Ivan the Terrible and Peter the Great (who, though responsible for much that was progressive, was also tyrannical in his methods) was carried on by Lenin and Stalin. In fact, it was only when the Soviet empire had a ruler at its head who was not prepared to resort to barbaric methods of controlling his subjects – Mikhail Gorbachev – that the system collapsed.

Russia was unique among the world's great empires, because the center and the colonies occupied a single territory. This made the empire far easier for Lenin and his successors to maintain, whilst trying to give the impression that the USSR was a voluntary union of independent peoples.

ABOVE RIGHT: Stalin's deportations of nationalities.

BELOW RIGHT: Mikhail Gorbachev on a visit to London in 1984.

ABOVE: Catherine the Great, Empress of Russia 1762-1796. Under Catherine, Russia achieved important victories against Persia and Turkey, including taking control of the Crimean peninsula.

RIGHT: An early Soviet propaganda poster in praise of the Third International.

LONG LIVE THE THIRD COMMUNIST INTERNATIONAL! EVVIVA IL TERZA INTERNAZIONALE COMMUNISTA! VIVE LA TROISIÈME INTERNATIONALE COMMUNISTE! ES LEBE DIE DRITTE KOMMUNISTISCHE INTERNATIONALE!

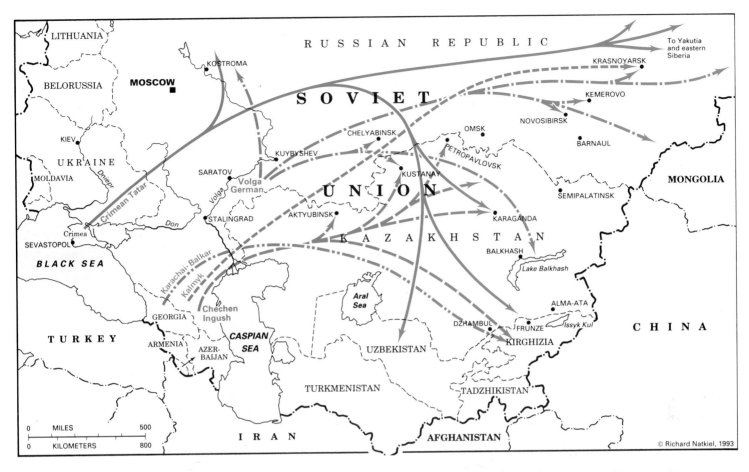

2
A NEW TYPE OF PARTY, A NEW TYPE OF STATE

LEFT: Karl Marx, the father of Communism.

RIGHT: The great Russian writer Fedor Dostoevsky, one of Russia's leading philosophers in the nineteenth century. Although exiled for his socialist beliefs, Dostoevsky ended up a staunch supporter of the monarchy.

BELOW: Peasants in the Nizhny Novgorod region in the late nineteenth century. The appalling conditions in which the peasantry lived inspired many intellectuals to want to improve their lot. But the peasants themselves were mistrustful of them.

In the latter part of the nineteenth century, discontent with the regime spread throughout the Russian empire. Ironically, discontent grew fastest at times when the heavy hand of the czar was lifted slightly. In comparison with his pre-decessors, Czar Alexander II was a moderate Russian leader. He saw better than any ruler before him the need for social change, though this did not go as far as relinquishing his auto-cratic powers.

Alexander II's main attempt at social reform was the emancipation of the serfs in 1861. Before this, the serfs on the land were the property of their masters; they could be bought and sold, ex-changed and abused, with no recourse to the law. Alexander hoped that emancipation would rid Russia of this feudalistic concept but, in reality, whilst emancipation helped some serfs, many suffered as a result. Disgruntled landlords refused to help their former 'slaves,' and thou-sands of serfs were left with no means of support at all. A fresh wave of anger swept across the country.

However, it was not among the peasantry that discontent was to develop into any coherent political ideas. With no political culture and, in many cases, no education, this would have been impossible. The first stirrings of political dissent came among the well-educated middle and upper classes. Much of this was referred to obliquely in the literature of the period. The image of the 'superfluous man' – Alexander Pushkin's Onegin, Mikhail Lermontov's Pecho-rin, Ivan Goncharov's Oblomov – came to symbolize the disillusioned gentry who felt their opportunities were stifled by the regime.

proponent of the ideology was Georgy Plekhanov; Lenin was to describe himself as being 'in love' with Plekhanov because of his political convictions. He was to be perhaps the only man whom Lenin ever continued to respect after falling out with him politically. Tolerance of political opponents was not a feature of Lenin's character.

Lenin was to develop the ideology of Marxism into Marxism-Leninism. Karl Marx had argued that history was a scientific process. Mankind had 'inevitably' developed from slavery to feudalism and then, as man's consciousness grew, from feudalism to capitalism. Each of these systems had been right for their time, but each had had its day. By the middle of the nineteenth century, Marx believed, capitalism was collapsing. Just as it had developed from feudalism, so, he theorized, it was now ripe to be replaced by socialism.

Marx recognized that this transition would not be peaceful. The capitalist bourgeoisie would not willingly give up their gains in order to improve the lives of the working masses. It would

In a society where open political criticism was impossible, perhaps it was inevitable that writers were to play a vital role in awakening people's political consciousness. Fedor Dostoevsky was sentenced to death (but granted a reprieve) for his political sins; Leo Tolstoy was excommunicated for offending the Orthodox Church, though given the importance of the Church in the running of the state, this was as much a political action as a religious one. Ivan Turgenev was particularly influential with his novel *Fathers and Sons*. Published in 1862, the book dealt not only with the age-old theme of the gap between generations, but more pointedly hinted at the gap between the old ideas of the regime and the progressive thoughts of the young. It was instrumental in establishing the destructive philosophy of nihilism (the total rejection of established laws and institutions).

One of the problems for the revolutionary movement as the nineteenth century drew to its close was that many of its ideas were exactly that: destructive. Furthermore, there was a distinct lack of coordination among the revolutionaries. The revolutionary acts which had taken place, such as the assassination of Czar Alexander II in 1881, had been sporadic. There was no concerted effort aimed at overthrowing the regime. Would-be revolutionaries seemed to spend more time squabbling among themselves than trying to find common ground on which to build the revolution.

There were already a few adherents of Marxism in Russia when the young Vladimir Ilych Ulyanov (Lenin's real name) began his political activity at Kazan University in 1887. The leading

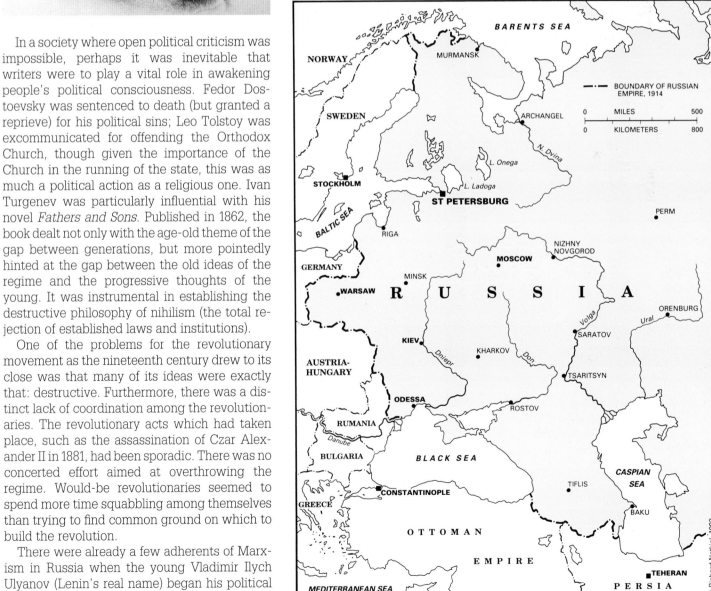

ABOVE: The assassination of Czar Alexander II, St Petersburg, March 1881.

LEFT: A statue of the young Lenin outside Kazan University.

come about only through revolution, but Marx never suggested how this might happen. The closest he came to a call for actual revolution was at the end of *The Communist Manifesto* which he wrote with Friedrich Engels in 1848. There, the declaration rang out which was to be on the masthead of Soviet newspapers throughout the years of Communist rule: 'Proletarians of All Countries Unite!' (It also adorned Marx's statue in Moscow. After the failed coup of August 1991, one wag with a can of spray-paint altered it to read 'Proletarians of All Countries – Forgive Me!')

By the turn of the century, Lenin had realized that a spontaneous, mass uprising of the workers would not happen. The proletariat's political awareness was, at best, in its infancy; for many it had still to be conceived. And even among his fellow revolutionaries, Lenin saw a lack of dedication to the cause which matched his own. Instead of pressing for political reform, both workers and revolutionaries were being distracted by what Lenin dubbed 'economism.' This meant that they were abandoning their goal of achieving political power for the workers in favor of promises of more money or better working conditions.

Lenin's main contribution to Communist theory evolved at this time. He began to see that economism could be defeated and revolution achieved only if the movement had a leader: the party. Like many of the revolutionaries, Lenin

was already a member of the Russian Social Democratic Labour Party (RSDLP), but differences between the members of the RSDLP came to a head at its second congress, held in Brussels and London in 1903. (Most of the party's activists were living abroad at this time because their political activity was illegal in Russia. Lenin himself had already spent three years in internal exile in Siberia.)

It was at the second congress that Lenin made it clear that he could no longer tolerate working alongside those whose dedication to the cause did not match his own fanaticism. What was needed, in Lenin's view, was 'a new type of party.' This would include only those who were prepared to fight actively for the cause; people who merely sympathized with its aims were excluded. This is why, throughout Soviet history, the Communist Party remained small. Membership rose as high as 19 million in 1988 but, as the population of the USSR at the time was 280 million, it was still less than seven percent of its citizens. The party was to be the vanguard of the working class, leading it to the revolution and creating a new type of state, guiding it through socialism and gradually withering away, with all the other organs of state, when Communism was achieved.

As a result of Lenin's intransigence, the crucial split in the RSDLP took place at the second congress. Lenin's group just managed to win a small majority before the split occurred, from which they claimed the title of 'majority-ists' – or Bolsheviks. The minority were given the somewhat derogatory term of 'minority-ists' – Mensheviks.

For the next 14 years, Lenin and the other Bolshevik leaders did most of their plotting for the revolution in exile. The spontaneous revolt which broke out in 1905, which is often thought

of as the first Russian revolution, caught them unawares. Russia was on the brink of an embarrassing defeat in the war against Japan when, on 22 January, a peaceful demonstration marched to the Winter Palace, the czar's residence in the capital, St Petersburg. Many of the marchers were living at near-starvation levels, and had decided as a last resort to call on Czar Nicholas II to help them. The march was met on Palace Square by armed soldiers, who opened fire. Over 70 people were killed, and the rest fled in panic. So delicate was the situation in society that unrest quickly spread in St Petersburg and then throughout the country.

The 1905 uprising lasted just a few months, though social turmoil in the form of strikes and labor unrest continued throughout the year. In August, Czar Nicholas made a political concession by opening a 'parliament,' the Duma. Though this was presented as a major advance in the growth of democracy in Russia, the Duma had little real power as it merely advised the czar, who still had the final say in everything.

The major achievement of the 1905 'revolution' was the change in the people's attitude toward the czar. That the people should have decided as a last resort to appeal to him illus-

LEFT: Friedrich Engels, co-author with Karl Marx of *The Communist Manifesto* in 1848.

BELOW: Czar Nicholas II (back left) and the Czarina Alexandra show off their first born, Olga, to Queen Victoria. The great royal families of Europe were all interrelated.

ABOVE: Leading members of the Bolshevik (majority) faction of the Russian Social Democratic Labor Party, following the split at the Party's Second Congress in 1903. Lenin is at top center (left), alongside his mentor, Georgy Plekhanov.

RIGHT: The Russo-Japanese War, 1904-1905. Russian soldiers defend a valley in Manchuria. The humiliations suffered in the war contributed to the outbreak of revolution in 1905.

trated the blind faith that many still retained in 'the Little Father,' as he was known. With all the social upheavals and growing poverty, the czar remained for many pure, but after his personal guard opened fire on the marchers – even though it is likely that the czar himself did not give the order – he was suddenly dragged down to a human, and, therefore, culpable level. This was to mean that, with the added despair of the military failures in World War I, the czar's abdication in March 1917 was not the great shock it would otherwise have been.

ABOVE: 9 January 1905. Russian officers on Palace Square in St Petersburg await marchers who were calling for the czar's intervention to alleviate their suffering. The demonstration was broken up when soldiers fired on the crowd. The day was christened Bloody Sunday, and sparked off the 1905 Revolution.

LEFT: Workers demonstrate on Nevsky Prospekt in St Petersburg during the 1905 Revolution.

The outbreak of war in August 1914 was at once an advantage and a disadvantage for the Bolsheviks. They saw it as a capitalist war, and therefore something with which the Russian working class had nothing in common. They hoped that this would inevitably lead to revolution, but had not reckoned with the strength of people's patriotism. Misguided or not, the

Russian workers came out in support of the war, and shunned or considered as traitors those who did not.

It was not until a series of calamities had left the Russian Army depleted and its morale shattered that mass disaffection with the war began. Riots in St Petersburg in February 1917 led, on 15 March, to Nicholas II heeding the counsel of his advisers and abdicating the throne. A Provisional Government, led by Alexander Kerensky and comprising representatives of many of the parties which had sprung up, took power. They even managed to gain support, at least initially, for their decision to continue the war.

Lenin did not support the Provisional Government, and saw it merely as a transitional stage in the march toward the formation of a Bolshevik government. He had returned to Russia in April and, with his platform of 'Bread! Land! Peace!', began to win greater support as the year, and the war, dragged on. In July the Bolsheviks thought their moment had come and tried to engineer an uprising against the Provisional Government. It failed, and Lenin was forced to flee across the border to Finland.

The Bolsheviks were not to make the same mistake again. The Provisional Government became increasingly unpopular, especially

because it refused to acknowledge the people's growing desire for Russia to leave the war. The Bolsheviks began to spread their influence among the workers, particularly in Petrograd (the capital was renamed after the outbreak of the war as St Petersburg sounded too German) and Moscow; and among the soldiers at the front. The sailors of the Kronstadt naval base near Petrograd were to play a vital role, too.

It was a ship from Kronstadt, the *Aurora*, which was to give the signal for the revolution to begin on the night of 7 November. The Bolsheviks had positioned men at key positions in the city, so that when the gun fired they moved into

LEFT: The cruiser *Aurora* at anchor on the River Neva in Petrograd, just after firing the shot which signaled the start of the Bolshevik seizure of power on 7 November 1917.

BELOW: The summer of 1917, between the March and November Revolutions, was a turbulent period in Russia. Here, in July, demonstrators on Petrograd's Nevsky Prospekt flee after being fired upon.

action, seizing key buildings. The Winter Palace, for so long the symbol of czarist rule and now the home of the Provisional Government, was the main target. So surprised were its would-be defenders, that the Bolshevik seizure of power was carried out in an almost bloodless fashion. The new type of party was set to build its new type of state.

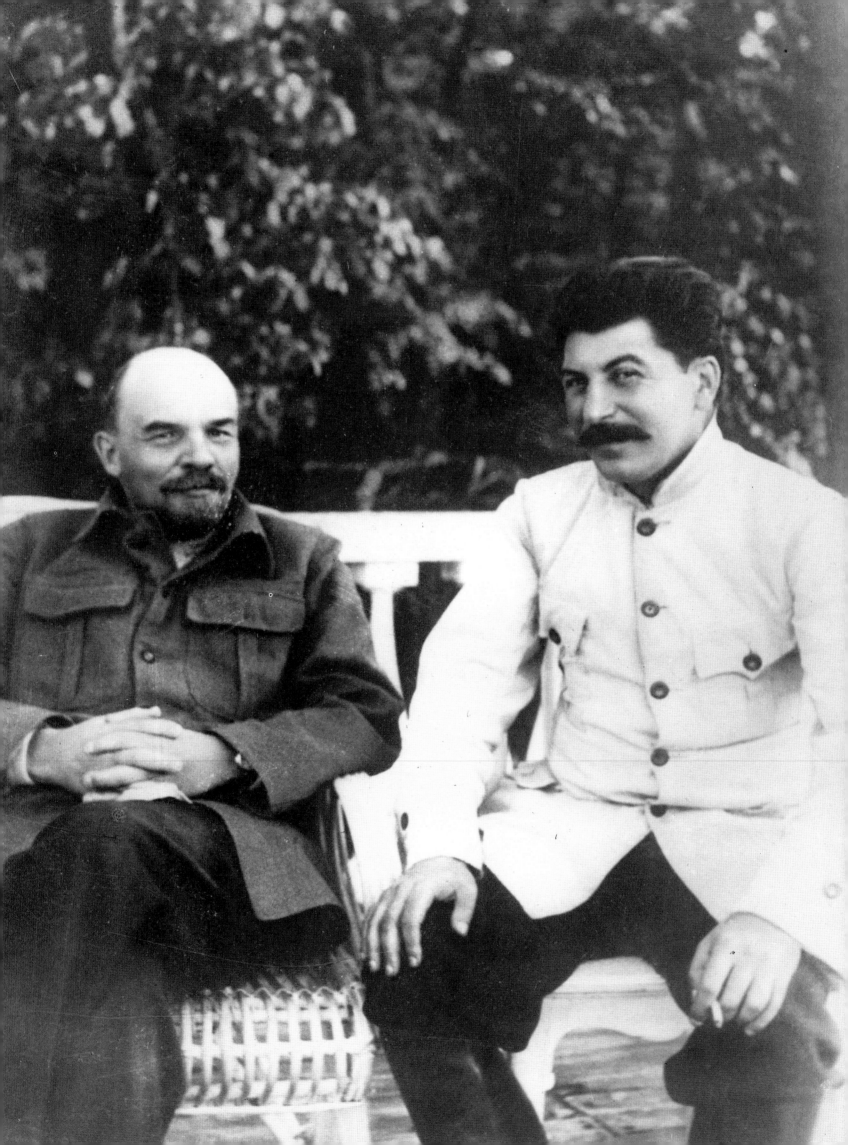

3
THE NEW EMPIRE

LEFT: Lenin at his rest home in Gorky, near
Moscow, is visited by Stalin in 1922.

When czarism was overthrown in the revolution of March 1917, many of the nationalities of the empire had high hopes for independence. For some, these expectations were heightened by the Bolshevik triumph in the November revolution that same year. After all, the Communist philosophy which the Bolsheviks preached was an internationalist one, and Lenin, the leader of the revolution, had described the Russian empire as 'the prison house of nationalities.'

The Bolsheviks considered the nationalities' question to be one of the most pressing matters facing them once they had seized power. On 15 November, just eight days after they had overthrown the Provisional Government, they passed the 'Declaration of the Rights of the Peoples of Russia.' This proclaimed the rights of all nations in the former empire to self-determination, up to and including the right to secede from Russia. In practice, however, the right of self-determination and, more especially, the right to secede, were to remain insignificant paper promises until the failed coup attempt in

August 1991 signaled the start of the break-up of the Soviet Union. But it would be wrong to dismiss this as pure cynicism on the part of the Bolshevik leadership. Rather, it illustrates the importance of Communist ideology in the early years of the Soviet state.

For Lenin, national boundaries were less important than class boundaries. In his mind, the working class of Russia had more in common with the working class of Germany, Britain or America than with the rulers of Russia who had been thrown out by the revolution. Though by the time of his death in 1924, he had become reconciled to the idea that the world revolution was not going to happen overnight, he still believed that the ultimate victory of socialism was not possible in a single country. Because Lenin saw the socialist revolution as a great leap forward for mankind along an inevitable historical path, it made no sense to him to allow the nations of the former Russian empire to break away from his revolution in order to form bourgeois capitalist states. So any question of bour-

BELOW: Symbol of a fallen dynasty. Children pose beside the head of the great statue of Czar Alexander III, felled in the Kremlin early in 1918.

geois nationalism was never meant to be included in the idea of self-determination for the non-Russian nationalities.

This was summed up by Joseph Stalin, whom Lenin appointed Commissar for Nationalities, when he addressed the Third All-Russian Congress of Soviets in January 1918. Events in Ukraine since the revolution had shown that nations gaining their independence from the old empire might not automatically take the socialist path, so Stalin clarified the point that the right of self-determination should be understood as the right 'not of the bourgeoisie but of the laboring masses of the given nation. The principle of self-determination should be a means in the struggle for socialism and should be subordinated to the principles of socialism.'

At the time, this point was ignored by many, either out of wishful thinking or because of a failure to grasp the internationalist nature of Communist ideology. As we shall see, this was to be a common failing over the decades that followed, as time and again Soviet leaders spelt out

LEFT: The young revolutionary Joseph Stalin. Stalin's real name was Djugashvili, but as with many of the revolutionaries he adopted a pseudonym. Stalin means 'man of steel.'

BELOW: Lenin watching the May Day parade on Moscow's Red Square in 1919. The woman looking on admiringly on the left of the picture is Lenin's wife, Nadezhda Krupskaya.

ABOVE: Stalin's police record card following his arrest for political agitation among the workers in Baku in 1908.

their belief that their system would triumph over capitalism, and then Western leaders would cry 'Foul!' when they suddenly realized that the norms under which they conducted foreign policy were not the same as those of the Soviet Union.

Before the Bolsheviks could decide any question of self-determination, they had to settle what it was that they actually controlled. When czardom collapsed and the Bolsheviks came to power, Russia was embroiled in World War I with Germany. Lenin was determined to extricate Russia from what he saw as a capitalist war as soon as possible. Negotiations for peace with Germany began a month after the revolution, on 9 December 1917, in the town of Brest-Litovsk (now on the Belorussian side of the border with Poland). Leon Trotsky, the leader of the Russian delegation, attempted to drag the talks out in the hope that Germany would be defeated by the Allies before agreement could be reached.

In the event, the Germans became fed up with the Russians' delaying tactics. They broke off the negotiations and the German Army advanced on the Russian capital, Petrograd. The Russians were forced back to the negotiating table, and the resulting peace treaty was undoubtedly harsher than it would have been three months earlier. Russia lost Finland, the Baltic

RIGHT: Leon Trotsky (second from left) leading the Russian delegation in the peace negotiations with Germany at Brest-Litovsk in December 1917.

States (Estonia, Latvia and Lithuania), its part of Poland, Belorussia and Ukraine. There were also concessions made to Turkey in the Caucasus. In terms of the percentage of the territory of the Russian empire these losses were significant though not great; but in terms of manpower, resources and cultivatable land, the treaty was a disaster.

After the German defeat in November 1918, Russia attempted to reverse the Treaty of Brest-Litovsk, but met with limited success. It succeeded in establishing a government in Belorussia, but lost its territories on the Baltic Sea. Ukraine was won back only because Poland chanced its arm too far. The Polish Army invaded Ukraine, capturing Kiev, but the Red Army managed to push the Poles out. After an ill-advised attempt to take Warsaw for the Bolsheviks, peace was finally made between the two sides with the Treaty of Riga signed in March 1921.

The other factor which was to decide the shape of the new Soviet state was the Civil War, which broke out in spontaneous opposition to the Bolsheviks all over the country. Some of this was inspired by nationalities trying to put self-determination into practice; but in other cases the opposition was united by nothing stronger than a desire to overthrow the Bolsheviks. Ultimately, the Bolsheviks' unity was to prove a

decisive factor. The Civil War also gave the Bolsheviks the chance to crush nationalist movements in some areas.

Тов. Ленин ОЧИЩАЕТ землю от нечисти.

LEFT: Post-revolutionary cartoon, entitled 'Comrade Lenin cleans the earth of the unclean.' A smiling Lenin is shown sweeping away the monarchy, the Church and the Capitalists, the three groups seen as the tormentors of the working class.

BELOW: The signing of the Treaty of Brest-Litovsk with Germany in 1918. Russian attempts to stall in December 1917 caused the Germans to lose patience and impose a much harsher treaty than would have been the case. But the Soviet Union was to reverse parts of the treaty after the German defeat in November 1918, and the rest of it following the Nazi-Soviet Pact of 1939.

ABOVE: German guards fighting the Bolsheviks in Riga (Latvia) during the Civil War.

BELOW: Lenin addressing a crowd in Sverdlov Square in Moscow in May 1920, at the height of the Civil War.

In Ukraine, the Bolsheviks used the anti-socialist nature of the provisional government as a pretext for driving it out and imposing their will. A Ukrainian Central Council, the Rada, had been established after the March revolution. Initially favoring Ukrainian autonomy within a decentralized Russia, the Rada supported the Whites (anti-Bolshevik forces) when the Civil War broke out. The Polish invasion of 1920 gave the Bolsheviks the pretext they needed to drive both the Poles and the Whites out of Ukraine. This was to leave bitter memories, and it is small wonder that the invading German Army in 1941 was to find a warm welcome in some parts of Ukraine.

The loss of territory in Transcaucasia was, indirectly, to be overturned by the victory of Kemal Ataturk in the Turkish revolution that followed the collapse of the Ottoman Empire in World War I. Russia and Turkey were now united in their opposition to the West. Furthermore, Turkey was in no position to resist Russia's determination to win back its losses in the region. In April 1920, the Red Army invaded Azerbaijan, which had recently gained its independence from Russia. The operation was planned to coincide with the uprising of Russian Bolsheviks resident in Baku from the time of the empire. Then in May, in one of the most cynical acts of the young Soviet republic, the Bolshevik government recognized the independence of the Republic of Georgia.

The Bolsheviks never intended Georgia to remain independent. It would have been anathema to permit a Menshevik – and thus, by definition, 'enemy' – government in territory which they considered as their own. Furthermore, Stalin, whose influence in the party was growing, was Georgian. It would have been too galling for the former Commissar for Nationalities to

belong to a nation which had rejected Bolshevism. At Stalin's encouragement, the Red Army invaded Georgia in February 1921, ostensibly at 'the invitation' of the Georgians.

This was to be a term used throughout Soviet history to justify the use of force. It was used for the last time as an excuse for sending tanks into Lithuania in January 1991. On this, as on every occasion before, it never seemed to bother the Soviet government that the person or persons that they claimed issued the invitation had no authority to do so in the first place.

In November 1920 Armenia had been seized by the Red Army. So by early 1921, Transcaucasia was established as a part of what was to be declared the Union of Soviet Socialist Republics the following year. The brutal crushing of uprisings in Armenia (1921) and Georgia (1924) served to emphasize this fact. By now Central Asia was also under Soviet control. The Bolsheviks had taken advantage of the sizeable Russian population in the city of Tashkent to assume control immediately after the revolution. Opposition remained in the surrounding countryside, and a

ABOVE: March 1919. Members of the Siberian bicycle and autocycle squad in Irkutsk. The squad was designed to be able to move swiftly from one trouble spot to another in the Civil War.

LEFT: Peasant victims of the Civil War.

RIGHT: Soldiers of the Whites fighting the Bolsheviks in Siberia in 1920.

BELOW: Young Communists sent to the villages as propagandists for the Bolshevik idea of amalgamating farms into collectives.

local provisional government was even established in Kokand, but this was broken up by the Bolsheviks in February 1918.

Soviet policy in Central Asia in the years after the revolution was in many ways a continuation of Imperial Russian policy. These were poor, educationally-backward areas of the old empire, something the Bolsheviks took full advantage of. In fairness, it must be said that their policy was not solely one of exploitation. Soviet power did bring advantages to Central Asia, especially in the fields of education and health care. But Islam, the religion of the area, was suppressed far more than it had been under the old regime, because atheism was an inherent part of Marxist-Leninist teaching. The redistribution of land favored immigrant Russian farmers more than the local population.

Administratively, Central Asia was initially organized into two union republics – Uzbekistan and Turkmenistan – and three autonomous republics, Kazakhstan, Kirghizia and Tajikistan. (In the 1930s, the last three were upgraded to full union status.) This was a classic example of divide and rule by the Soviet government. Historically and culturally, the Uzbeks, the Turkmen and the Kirghiz were very close but, by creating a number of different nations, the Soviet government's aim was to destroy any sense of common identity and to control their mutual relations by way of Moscow. The success of this policy was evident after the coup in 1991, when the Central Asian republics showed themselves the least prepared of all the republics for independence.

Despite the mix of nationalities within the newly-proclaimed Russian federation, there were few anti-Bolshevik stirrings generated by the desire for national self-determination. A notable exception was in the Tatar homeland, around the city of Kazan. A Moslem assembly (Medzhlis) was set up in Kazan in February 1918, and preparations were made to create a Volga-Ural autonomous state in the Russian heartland.

Just as the Bolsheviks could not tolerate bourgeois nationalism, so they were not prepared to allow self-determination based largely on religious grounds. The Red Army took Kazan, the Medzhlis was suppressed and the Tatar-Bashkir Soviet Republic was proclaimed in March. This included a lot of small national groups, as well as a large number of Russians, which meant that neither the Tatars nor the Bashkirs represented a majority. Czech interventionists seized the area later in 1918, but after they had been driven out, the area was split into six smaller regions, designated as autonomous union republics.

During the 1920s, when the New Economic Policy (NEP) was in force, the nationalities did not suffer open persecution. In fact, of the two 'deviations' which Communists were told to avoid – 'Great Russian' chauvinism and local bourgeois nationalism – more energy was devoted to the former than the latter. In Ukraine, Ukrainian became the language used in schools and business. Similarly, in the Tatar Autonomous Republic, the Tatar language was more widely used than it had been at any time since Ivan the Terrible had captured the city in 1552. Russia even became the only union republic without its own Communist Party. When the Russian Party became the All-Union Party in 1925, it was decided that there should not be a Russian Party, since by its very size it would rival, and probably dominate, the All-Union Party. (The Russian Communist Party was reformed only in June 1990, but was disbanded

RIGHT: Stalin among deputies to the First Congress of collective farmers in Moscow in 1933. On Stalin's right is Kliment Voroshilov, a future Marshal of the Soviet Union and one of the few senior military officers to survive Stalin's purges in the late Thirties.

BELOW: For a country which was desperately backward in its agricultural methods, the tractor came to symbolize Soviet power in the countryside. Children were called 'Tractor' in its honor. These Uzbek peasants in Samarkand are being given lessons in new farming methods.

along with all the other branches of the party after the failed coup in August 1991.

Things were to change when NEP ended in 1928, to be replaced by the collectivization of agriculture and the first five-year plan. At the same time, the Soviet leadership committed itself to building 'socialism in one country,' temporarily putting aside the goal of world Communism. Since spontaneous revolutions had not happened in the wake of the Bolshevik victory in

Russia, it was considered vital to ensure that socialism established a firm base in the world's only socialist state, from where the revolution could then be spread in the future.

Although the whole Soviet population was to fall further and further under the rule of fear imposed by Stalin, the nationalities were to suffer especially. It is a bitter irony that the man responsible was not even Russian, but Georgian. As Lenin himself had said prophetically of Stalin in 1922, 'it is well-known that Russified people of foreign birth always overshoot themselves in the matter of the true Russian disposition.'

Collectivization was to hit Ukraine and Central Asia particularly hard. Because of the determination of the Ukrainian peasants to hang on to their private smallholdings, the Red Army was sent in to commandeer crops and livestock and enforce the process. In the severest of lessons, Stalin deliberately created famine in the republic in 1932 and 1933. To this day, it is not known how many millions of peasants died as a result.

In Kazakhstan, the Soviet government set about putting an end to the centuries-old nomadic lifestyle of the local people by forcing them into permanent agricultural settlements. The result was famine, the mass destruction of livestock, and the death of about one-third of the republic's population. In neighboring Turkmenistan, the losses of livestock were so great that in 1933 the republic had just one-fifth of the number of cattle that it had had four years earlier.

After a brief lull in the mid-Thirties, the nationalities were to feel Stalin's wrath during the 'purges,' especially between 1936 and 1939. As with collectivization, it was not only the nationalities who suffered. Millions of innocent Russians also perished or languished for years in the labor camps, but the effect of the purges on the nationalities was arguably even more devastating. Initially directed against the Communist Party and fueled by Stalin's paranoia that there were plots against him everywhere, the purges also provided Stalin with a chance to Russify the country further. For example, in Ukraine the whole of the republican party's ruling Politburo disappeared, and four-fifths of the Central Committee. Many of these were replaced by Russians.

One thing lacking in the first 20 years or so after the revolution was any concerted effort to spread the message worldwide. This would have disappointed the early theorists of Communism. Even Lenin before the revolution believed that it would need worldwide action to keep it alive. In 1919 the Third International, the Comintern, was formed for this purpose. Although the Russians championed the cause of the Comintern with grand words, in practice they were too concerned with ensuring the stability of their own state to make any concerted effort to use it to spread Communism westward.

The only other Communist-run state established throughout the whole period was Mongolia, where Communists seized power with the help of the Red Army in July 1921. Although Russian influence over Mongolia grew in the Twenties, the country remained independent and, in terms of the Soviet empire, was a role model for the countries of Eastern Europe after World War II – self-governing, but Soviet-dominated.

The history of the Soviet state between the revolution and the outbreak of war in Europe in 1939 divides into two parts. In the 1920s, there was still debate over which direction the revolution should take, and concepts such as the New Economic Policy, which allowed limited capitalism, were permitted. From the time that 'socialism in one country' was adopted at the end of the Twenties, Stalin's principal aim was consolidation of the gains already made. In 1939, history dictated that the time had come to begin the process of spreading the revolution.

ABOVE: The ultimate socialist realist statue, depicting the mighty worker with his hammer, and the strong peasant woman with her sickle: the encapsulation of the workers' and peasants' state. Standing on the edge of the Exhibition of Economic Achievements of the USSR, both the statue and the Exhibition have become ironic symbols of failure for many Russians.

4
THE EMPIRE EXPANDS

LEFT: The Soviet flag is raised over the
Reichstag in Berlin, May 1945. This was to
symbolize both victory over Germany and the
start of the expansion of the Soviet empire into
Eastern Europe.

The Nazi-Soviet Pact of August 1939 exploded like a bombshell. Here were the two sworn ideological enemies, Fascism and Communism, not only publicly declaring that they would not attack each other, but swearing their friendship. Surely this negated any idea that Marxism-Leninism could still be considered a viable ideology?

In fact, to the orthodox Communist, there was nothing wrong with the basic idea of signing an agreement with Nazi Germany which would guarantee the security of socialism. The Nazi-Soviet Pact is the perfect example of how conventional 'bourgeois' concepts of morality, cannot be applied to Communism. Communism's grand strategy was to triumph worldwide. In order to achieve this, different tactics would have to be applied to suit the prevailing circumstances. Even if these tactics – like the Nazi-Soviet Pact – seemed to contradict the ideology in the short-term, when viewed in their long-term context of securing Communism's future they make sound ideological sense.

What was inexcusable for many Communists was the declaration of friendship with Hitler which went with the pact. Even in ideological terms this was both unnecessary and impossible to justify. It helped to shelve any hopes for the spreading of the revolution worldwide, since Communist parties which were loyal to Moscow – and thus were finding their policies difficult to support anyway – now lost all credibility.

In practical terms, though, the Nazi-Soviet Pact gave Stalin the first opportunity to extend the boundaries of the empire. This had two purposes. The first was to restore to Russia territories in Eastern Europe which had formerly belonged to the old empire. The second showed the shallowness of the pact. Although under its terms Russia and Germany agreed not to attack each other for at least 10 years, neither Stalin nor Hitler believed that the pact would last its course. By obtaining territory in Eastern Europe, Stalin acquired a buffer zone with which he hoped to protect 'Mother Russia.' If he were to have less time than he anticipated – as proved to be the case – immediately after the pact was signed, Stalin planned to move Soviet heavy industry east of the Ural Mountains.

The first country to suffer from what, for Stalin, was the re-adjustment of the losses of the Treaty of Brest-Litovsk, was Poland. The Nazi-Soviet Pact was signed on 23 August 1939. Nine days later, on 1 September, Germany invaded Poland from the west. On 3 September, Britain and France declared war on Germany. A week later, the Red Army crossed Poland's eastern border, and divided the country with Germany along a line agreed in their pact.

The people of the three Baltic States, Estonia, Latvia and Lithuania, also had cause to fear. The Soviet government concluded pacts of 'military assistance' with the legal governments of these countries. In June 1940, there were Soviet-backed political coups in each of the states, which were to be described in later Soviet mythology as 'invitations' to the Soviet Union for assistance. After just 21 years of independence, they became union republics of the USSR.

RIGHT: August 1939, two ideological enemies become friends. German Foreign Minister von Ribbentrop (left) and Soviet Commissar for Foreign Affairs Molotov (right) have just signed the Nazi-Soviet Non-Aggression Pact. Stalin and Gaus, German Under-Secretary of State, look on approvingly. The Pact also contained the secret protocols under which the two countries divided up Poland between them, and Russia regained the Baltic States of Estonia, Latvia and Lithuania, as well as Moldavia from Rumania.

In the same month, Stalin felt confident enough to demand of Rumania the return of Bessarabia, which Lenin had given up in 1918, and also the adjacent province of North Bukovina, which had not been part of the czarist empire. Rumania felt unable to resist. The only area where the Russians met genuine resistance to the agreed annexations of the Nazi-Soviet Pact was Finland. Shortly after the occupation of Poland, Stalin entered into negotiations with Finland. Here, as in Poland and Rumania, his intention was to take back former bits of the empire, as well as establish a protective zone, in this case around his second city, Leningrad. In November 1939 negotiations broke down. War seemed inevitable. On 30 November the Red Army attacked Finland.

This should have been a swift campaign. The Finns were no match for the might of the Red Army. Although the Soviet side won, it was not an easy victory as the Finns defended their land bravely. The terrain was difficult and the campaign was conducted in harsh winter conditions. The Red Army had suffered badly in Stalin's purges, it had lost many of its best commanders and morale was low. The Winter War, as it became known, dragged on for four months. Although Stalin made the territorial gains that he wanted at the start of the campaign, the Soviet Union was castigated by world opinion – it was

expelled from the League of Nations – and guaranteed that Finland would fight on Germany's side in the invasion of the USSR which was soon to come.

Despite Stalin's mistrust of Hitler, notwithstanding the Nazi-Soviet Pact, the German invasion of the Soviet Union in the early hours of 22

ABOVE: German soldiers smash Polish border posts, 1 September 1939.

BELOW: Molotov is given full state honors as he leaves Berlin in 1940.

RIGHT: Despite the Nazi-Soviet Pact, on 22 June 1941 Germany invaded the Soviet Union. The USSR lost an estimated 20 million people over the next four years. This scene, in Kerch in the Crimea, as parents come across the dead body of their son, was repeated over and over again.

BELOW: In the early weeks of the war, the Germans completely overran the unprepared Red Army. Here captured Red Army soldiers are searched for weapons.

June 1941 caught the Soviet leader unprepared. Stalin had chosen to ignore reliable intelligence reports in the weeks before the attack, some of which gave the exact date it was to be launched.

The extent of the unpreparedness is illustrated by reports from the frontline. Coming under German fire at 0400 hours, one border post engaged in the following bizarre exchange:

'We are being attacked! What shall we do?'

'You must be insane. And why was your message not in code?'

It was not just the German attack for which Stalin was unprepared. He also did not expect that in some of the USSR's western regions the Germans would be welcomed as liberators. This euphoria was not to last. As the Nazis treated all Slavs as *untermenschen* (lesser beings) they quickly lost what sympathy they had, but the initial attitude to the Germans was to rekindle Stalin's paranoia that he was surrounded by potential enemies. The occupation of Poland and the Baltic States had been followed by the mass deportation of 'unreliable elements' to Central Asia and Siberia. With the war now in progress, Stalin began similar deportations of a number of national groups which had long been part of the Empire.

The first to suffer in this way were the ethnic Germans living in the lower Volga basin. Although still classified as 'Germans,' these people were the descendants of settlers who had come from Germany at the invitation of Empress Catherine in the eighteenth century. Now, their distant national roots were enough for Stalin to

consider them Nazi sympathizers, and 400,000 were forcibly deported to Central Asia and Siberia. A similar fate befell the Crimean Tatars, the Kalmyks of the Caspian steppes and four nations in the Caucasus: the Chechens, the Ingush, the Balkars and the Karachays. In all, about 1.5 million people were herded off to the less hospitable parts of the USSR on Stalin's whim. Their alleged crime was that they had shown insufficient support for the Soviet war effort. Not only did this mean that some elements within the national group had shown sympathy or open support for the Germans, but also that the majority were being punished for not denouncing such people.

Apart from causing deep grief and great human suffering – something which seems never to have bothered Stalin – the mass deportations during World War II were to have serious repercussions in the aftermath of the break-up of the Soviet Union in 1991. The Autonomous Republic of Chechen-Ingushetia was the first part of Russia to claim independence from Moscow, with the Chechen majority dominating the Ingush. The thorny problem of whether Crimea was a part of Ukraine, a part of Russia, or independent was complicated in April 1992 when the Ukrainian President, Leonid Kravchuk, invited the Crimean Tatars to return to their homeland. The small Tatar minority already there

were supporters of Crimea remaining a part of Ukraine. Around the same time, it was agreed that with German assistance a German Autonomous Republic would be re-established on the Volga. Although this was more inspired by a German desire to stem the flow of immigrants from Russia, it was bound to lead to tensions among the existing population of the area.

Another part of Stalin's legacy was to cause serious problems 50 years later in the southwest

ABOVE: For many, the Soviet victory at the Battle of Stalingrad in 1943 was the turning point of the war. The relief of the local people is evident here as they welcome their liberators.

LEFT: In 1943 'The Big Three' – Stalin, Roosevelt and Churchill – met for the first time in Tehran, to plan the defeat of Germany and postwar strategy. But the wartime alliance was not to survive the ideological struggle that peace renewed.

ABOVE: An exhibition of German equipment captured by the Russians after the Battle of Leningrad. Leningrad was under siege for 900 days, but managed to hold out; an estimated one and a half million Leningraders died. Hitler was so confident he would take the city that he even had invitations printed for a victory celebration in the Astoria Hotel.

of the country. Having retaken Bessarabia from Rumania, Stalin added to it Trans-Dniester to create the Soviet republic of Moldavia. Trans-Dniester had never been a part of Rumania, and was populated largely by Slavs. When the break-up of the USSR was imminent, the area declared its independence from Moldavia, its leaders citing fears that Moldavia was to rejoin Rumania. This became one of the main ethnic

trouble spots on the territory of the former Soviet Union.

As fears of what had seemed like certain defeat at the hands of the Germans began to fade, notably after the German surrender at Stalingrad in February 1943, Stalin began to make plans for the new, 'second' empire which he was to rule when the war was over. Although he declared the Nazi-Soviet Pact to be null and void shortly after the German invasion of 1941, he also insisted that the Soviet Union's western borders be recognized as those that existed at the time of the attack. This determination to hang on to the gains made by the 'secret proto-cols' to the Nazi-Soviet Pact was to be Stalin's consistent, and eventually successful, position in negotiations with the Allies at the two war-time summit conferences at Tehran and Yalta, and the postwar one at Potsdam.

Stalin wanted more than simply a larger Soviet Union: he also wanted to establish control over those parts of Eastern Europe which would come under Soviet domination as his troops swept westward to Berlin. In the first place, this would give the USSR the buffer it wanted to pre-vent a repeat of the surprise German attack in the future. Just as Stalin had known that the Pact with Hitler was only a temporary alliance of mutual convenience, so he recognized that the accommodation with the Western Allies was un-likely to last long once the common enemy of Germany was defeated.

RIGHT: Allies join hands. Russian and American soldiers meet at Torgau on the River Elbe in April 1945. Such scenes were soon to become distant memories when the Cold War began.

Whilst relations were still good, though, Stalin was determined to gain as much as he could. In August 1945, he declared war on Japan. As one of the victorious powers when Japan surrendered in the same month, the Soviet Union was able to take back the southern half of the Sakhalin peninsula, which had been ceded to Japan after Russia's defeat in the war of 1905, and occupy the two northernmost Kurile Islands. These had been recognized by Russia in 1875 as being Japanese. Japan refused to sign a peace treaty with the USSR until they were returned, a policy it maintained even after the collapse of the Soviet Union.

There was also the desire – however cynical it might seem in the post-Communist era – to spread Communism. In fact, it was this aspect, in a disguised form, which became the *raison d'etre* for the creation of the second empire in Eastern Europe. Once Soviet rule had been re-established in those territories which Stalin had gained under the terms of the secret protocols, the Soviet Union began a meticulous process of establishing its rule in Eastern Europe, whilst at the same time giving that rule an air of authority. The establishment of Moscow's regimes in Poland, Czechoslovakia, Hungary, Rumania, Bulgaria and what was to become East Germany followed a common pattern, even though the political situation in each country differed in its readiness for the introduction of a Soviet-type system.

Immediately after the war was over, coalition governments were established in which the Communist or pro-Communist party was one group among others. The influence of the Communists was then increased. Communist ideas and parties were given prominence, and non-Communist views were suppressed within parliament. Finally, opposition outside parliament and to the now-Communist government was silenced. By the end of 1948 this process was complete. Almost 50 years later, and having witnessed how swiftly Communism collapsed in Eastern Europe, it seems hard to believe that such changes could be forced in just three years, but that is to ignore the circumstances of the time.

Firstly, Stalin had succeeded in getting the tacit approval of the Western Allies that he had virtually a free hand in those territories won back from Fascism by the Red Army. Secondly, the will of those Allies to continue the fight was highly questionable. Britain had been at war for six years, and the United States for four and, since 1941, the USSR had been an ally in the fight against Nazi Germany. The shock caused by the Nazi-Soviet Pact had largely been erased by the enormous sacrifice which the Soviet Union had made in expelling the Germans: the final death total was to be 20 million. Added to these factors was an acute understanding within the Soviet leadership of what had to be done in each of the countries which fell under its control.

BELOW: Russian prisoners-of-war freed by the Americans from a camp at Eselheide.

Soviet plans for Poland were helped by the Warsaw Uprising of August to October 1944. The Soviet leadership encouraged the Polish resistance in Warsaw to rise up against the Germans when Soviet troops were only a short distance from the city. The Soviet version of what happened next was that no guarantees were given to the resistance and it was merely unfortunate for them that the Soviet forces had to stop short of Warsaw in order to regroup and await supplies. To the Poles this has always been a cynical example of a deliberate Soviet policy to ensure that the most able leaders of the resistance were wiped out by the Germans, thereby preventing them from being in a position to form an effective opposition to the Communists after the Soviet take-over.

Of all the countries of Eastern Europe, Czechoslovakia was the only one which could be described as a parliamentary democracy before the war. Ironically, this meant that the Communist Party there was stronger than in any of the other countries. When the initial coalition government was established after the war, many of the Communist politicians within it already had practical experience of politics, which eased their take-over of the government. Soviet troops

were withdrawn from Czechoslovakia at the end of 1945, but they remained in Hungary, Rumania and Bulgaria because these countries had been allies of Germany. They were to act as a coercive force in the establishment of Communist power. Bulgaria had actually experienced its own Communist revolution in September 1944, after which the new government sided with the Soviet Union.

Another factor peculiar to Bulgaria was that this fellow-Slav country had strong historical links with Russia. The most important example was the aid the Russians had given to liberate Bulgaria from the Turks in 1878. Soviet 'help' in consolidating the results of the Bulgarian revolution of 1944 was presented as an example of history repeating itself.

The Red Army, or the Soviet Army as it was renamed after the war, also stayed in Poland, in order to effect reliable communications with the army of occupation in the Soviet-run sphere of Germany. With the benefit of hindsight it is clear that once Germany – and, in miniature, the capital, Berlin – was divided between the victorious Allies (the USA, Britain, France and the USSR) there was no doubt that a socialist system would be applied to the Soviet sector. Stalin

BELOW: Lieutenant-General Kazma Derezyanko signs the Japanese surrender document for the Soviet Union on board the USS *Missouri* in 1945. The USSR's major gain was the Kurile Islands, a move which was to prevent Japan from ever signing a peace treaty with the Soviet Union.

genuinely feared that a unified Germany could again be a threat to the security of the Soviet Union, and so had no intention of even contemplating allowing close ties between East and West.

By the end of the 1940s Stalin had succeeded in a two-part expansion of the empire. He had taken back many of the territories which had been part of the czarist empire but had been lost after World War I and the revolution. His grip over these lands was unquestionable. The powerful NKVD (the People's Commissariat for Internal Affairs, the predecessor of the KGB) ensured that fear kept under control any desire to be different, be it inspired by politics or nationalism. Stalin also showed that he was prepared to resort to mass deportations again when he turned his attention to his native republic, Georgia, in 1948. Thousands of Georgians were shipped to Central Asia on no more than a suspicion of anti-Soviet beliefs.

Stalin now also had his second empire in Eastern Europe. This was controlled less by the troops that were stationed throughout much of its territory than by the setting-up of political systems which mirrored the Soviet one. The government of each country was merely a rubber

stamp for the decisions of the Communist Party, even if the ruling party was entitled 'Socialist' or 'People's,' rather than Communist. Whilst Stalin was in power, Moscow's grip on Eastern Europe could not be questioned, but after his death in March 1953, the first tiny signs began to show that this empire had not come into existence by the will of its peoples.

ABOVE: A German doctor performs an autopsy on a Polish soldier in Katyn Forest, 1943.

BELOW: Soviet troops are welcomed in Prague, Czechoslovakia, in 1945.

5
THE SECOND EMPIRE REBELS

LEFT: Hungarians defending a radio station in Budapest during the uprising against the Soviet Army in November 1956.

Whilst Stalin was alive, any serious attempt to overthrow the system, either from inside or outside the Soviet Union, would have been doomed to failure. The system relied on a climate of fear which meant that any citizen holding views which dissented from the official line tended to keep them to himself. Many of those who failed to do this simply disappeared without trace. Thus it was that the essential element for maintaining the Communist system was established: not a mass belief in the principles of Marxism-Leninism, but wholesale fear that any attempt to step out of line would be met by swift and harsh punishment.

Events in Eastern Europe, 'the second empire,' from the time of Stalin's death in March 1953 until 1968, were to show that, on the one hand, this Stalinist method of maintaining the system had been relaxed, since protest voices were heard, but on the other hand it could not be dispensed with entirely. This was first illustrated in East Germany, just three months after Stalin died.

The marked difference between the attitudes of the victorious Allies after World War II was illustrated by their behavior in the zones of Germany where their troops were stationed. In the West, the Americans in particular set about restoring the German economy, whilst ensuring that the country did not develop its military might again. After the formation of the North

Atlantic Treaty Organization (NATO) in 1949, and especially after the Federal Republic of Germany (FRG) became a member in 1955, it was clear that the reason that American, British and other NATO forces were stationed in West Germany was because that country was in the front-line of any possible clash with the Soviet Union. They did not form an army of occupation.

In the German Democratic Republic (GDR), however, the Soviet Army was an army of occupation. Furthermore, the Soviets were determined to make the country pay for the devastating losses that the USSR had suffered at German hands in the war. As a result, much of the country's wealth was shipped back to the Soviet Union as reparations, and the standard of living of the East German people was deliberately kept low. The Socialist Unity Party (SED) could be relied upon to carry out Moscow's wishes, largely because many of its leaders had lived in the USSR and, in any case, Soviet troops were never far away should they be needed. Moscow judged that they were needed on 17 June 1953, the first time that Soviet tanks were used to crush an uprising outside the USSR.

The factor which sparked off the East German uprising of June 1953 was the SED's decision to increase work quotas. What this meant was that a labor force which was already working under tough conditions was asked to do more for less in terms of real wages. Petitions calling on the

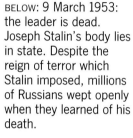

BELOW: 9 March 1953: the leader is dead. Joseph Stalin's body lies in state. Despite the reign of terror which Stalin imposed, millions of Russians wept openly when they learned of his death.

LEFT: Stalin's coffin is borne on a gun carriage to his resting place in the mausoleum beside Lenin. His successor as Party leader, Nikita Khrushchev (seen far right), was to denounce Stalin's crimes in 1956. In 1961 Stalin's body was removed from the mausoleum and buried in the Kremlin Wall.

party to rescind the work quotas were first drawn up on 15 June in East Berlin. When this met with no response from the authorities, the workers decided to march on government headquarters the next day. By the time the march reached its goal, it numbered an estimated 10,000 – a huge display of discontent in a country where such protests just did not happen.

The protest was once again ignored by the authorities. This led to a crucial shift in the workers' demands. Whereas they had until now restricted their protest to the question of the work quotas, calls for political changes were now heard, notably for the resignation of the SED leader Walter Ulbricht and for free elections. An urgent appeal went out for a general strike. This spread quickly throughout the country, largely because the message was picked up and broadcast by West German radio, which was easily received in the East.

BELOW: The first uprising against Soviet rule in Eastern Europe came on 17 June 1953 in Berlin. It was swiftly put down by Soviet tanks.

ABOVE: East Berliners smash down signs marking the border between the Soviet and American sectors.

BELOW: A newsstand burns.

some 25,000 men – were to be deployed in the city.

As the morning wore on, the situation became more volatile. SED banners were burned and its property smashed. By one o'clock in the afternoon, matters had come to such a head that the Soviet Military Commandant in Berlin, Major-General Dibrova, declared martial law in the city. The first deaths had already occurred, as Soviet armored vehicles drove into crowds of demonstrators. By the end of the day the revolt had been ended, as people obeyed the curfew imposed under martial law. The Soviets had already shown that they would not hesitate to shoot those violating it.

The strike call had been taken up by some 300,000 workers in nearly 300 towns and cities throughout the GDR. Given the swift deployment of Soviet troops, it is remarkable that the death toll remained low – 25 according to official East German statistics. Even Western estimates were not a great deal higher. Although protests, and even strikes, continued sporadically in the weeks that followed, the mass demonstration was over.

For the Soviet authorities, matters had gone too far. The first tanks took up positions on the streets of Berlin early on the morning of 17 June. This in itself did not deter the workers, however. By seven o'clock in the morning thousands had already flocked into the center of East Berlin. In the course of the day, two motorized divisions –

The lessons of 17 June were there for all to see. The party was not omnipotent: it had to back down over the issue of work quotas, so from that point of view the workers had been successful.

But the real lesson was that the Soviet Union considered Eastern Europe to be its empire, and that no attempt to alter the status quo in that empire would be tolerated.

This lesson was to be confirmed in Hungary three years later, despite signs from the Soviet authorities that they were determined to move away from the excesses of Stalinism. Nikita Khrushchev's so-called 'secret speech' to the Twentieth Congress of the Soviet Communist Party in February 1956 seemed to be a graphic illustration of this policy, as he spoke of Stalin's crimes for the first time. The speech was delivered to a closed session of the party faithful. But it was deliberately leaked to the West. These admissions seemed to step up the 'New Course,' as it had been dubbed. This caused confusion for Communists both in the Soviet Union and in Eastern Europe.

The first stirrings of discontent occurred in Poland in June 1956, when a peaceful uprising in Poznan led to the dismissal of Boleslaw Bierut as party leader and the appointment of Wladyslaw Gomulka. But it was in Hungary four months later that the real test came for the Soviet leadership. Growing discontent with the economic and political situation in the country erupted in a mass demonstration in Budapest on 23 October. In a highly significant gesture, the huge statue of

Stalin was toppled. The political crisis which had been brewing in the Hungarian leadership now spilled over. Imre Nagy, the former prime minister, who had been expelled from the party and the government in disgrace a year earlier, was now recalled. The move had Moscow's blessing.

ABOVE: A Hungarian displays a burning picture of Lenin.

BELOW: Signs of open defiance in Budapest.

RIGHT: Imre Nagy, recalled as Hungarian Prime Minister as the Budapest uprising intensified, addresses parliament on 24 October. When he declared Hungary's independence and proposed its withdrawal from the Warsaw Pact a week later, Nagy won the lasting admiration of the Hungarian people.

FAR RIGHT: Nothing symbolized the fear and desperation of the Soviet empire more than the Berlin Wall. Erected in 1961, it was ostensibly meant to keep out Westerners; in fact, as incidents such as this one show, it was there to keep East Germans in.

BELOW: A West Berlin woman waves across the Wall.

In the week that followed, Nagy tried to strike a balance which would satisfy both the Hungarian people and the Soviet leadership. He declared martial law, but also offered an amnesty to those who ceased fighting and handed over their weapons. He kept up a continuous dialogue with Moscow's envoys, Anastas Mikoyan and Mikhail Suslov, and also with the Soviet ambassador, Yuri Andropov (who was to become the head of the KGB from 1967 to 1982, and Soviet leader from November 1982 until his death in February 1984).

Nagy's efforts in that week were more successful with the Soviets than with his own people. His government was praised by Soviet leaders, but as the rebellion continued on the streets of Budapest and in other parts of the country, a repeated call was for the Soviets to leave Hungary. This goal seemed as if it might be realized, when it was announced on 29 October that Soviet Army units were to be withdrawn forthwith from Budapest.

The next day, as Soviet troops continued to leave Budapest, the Soviet government made public an official declaration stating that the USSR was prepared to review the question of its forces stationed in both Hungary and Rumania. On the same day, Nagy announced the formation of a multi-party coalition government, one of the main demands of the uprising. Still Moscow appeared satisfied. It seems that the Kremlin's patience snapped the next day. Events in Hungary were moving so far away from the Soviet model of Communism that there was a real fear that this 'counter-revolution,' as they saw it, could spread and 'infect' the other countries of the empire. Early on the morning of 1 November, Soviet troops crossed the Hungarian border. That same day, members of the Soviet leadership traveled to Brest (on the Soviet-Polish border) and Bucharest to inform the leaders of the other East European countries of their intention to crush the Hungarian uprising as swiftly as possible.

Andropov tried to reassure Nagy that the troops which were coming into Hungary were only there to ensure the safe passage of those leaving. Whilst some of the Hungarian people tried to reassure themselves that this was the case – after all, there were no longer any Soviet troops in Budapest – on the evening of 1 November Nagy declared Hungary's independence and its withdrawal from the Warsaw Pact (which had been formed only in 1955). He also appealed to the United Nations for help.

By this gesture, Nagy, the devoted Communist who had previously toed Moscow's line religiously, won a place in the hearts of his countrymen, but it made no difference to the Kremlin plan. Before dawn on 4 November, Soviet forces swooped on Budapest and other key cities. They seized important objectives such as airfields, bridges and freight yards, as well as the parliament building. Most Hungarians awoke to find that the uprising was effectively over.

Bernauer Straße

ABOVE: US President John F Kennedy and Soviet Foreign Minister Andrei Gromyko.

held until the following year, when he was returned, still a prisoner, to Budapest. On 16 June 1958, Nagy was executed. The people of Eastern Europe, and of the world, had seen that the Soviet Union was not prepared to allow any change from the course which it had set for the countries of its second empire. This lesson was to be repeated in Czechoslovakia in 1968. Before that, there was to be another graphic demonstration that the Soviet empire regarded itself as a besieged fortress. Besieged not in a military sense, but by the alien idea of freedom as understood in the capitalist West.

As the standard of living in the empire improved only gradually, and lagged well-behind that in the West, more and more people were choosing to leave. The easiest way to do this was through Berlin, which remained under the control of the four wartime Allies (the USA, Britain, France and the USSR). Although each power had been assigned a sector of the city, there was freedom of movement between them. This was having a destabilizing effect on East Germany in particular: by late 1959 over two million citizens had abandoned the GDR for life in the West, many of them skilled workers and professional

A pro-Soviet government was formed with the collusion of Janos Kadar, who had been in Nagy's emergency cabinet. Nagy himself was arrested and taken to Rumania, where he was

ABOVE: Alexander Dubcek.

BELOW LEFT: East German soldiers repair the Wall.

BELOW: Nicolae Ceausescu (third from right).

that East Berlin had been sealed off to protect it from the threat of attack from the West. The barricades, which were soon replaced by a high wall in the center of the city and a heavily-guarded fence around the border of West Berlin with the GDR, were there to keep people in. The removal of the Berlin Wall was to become the symbol of the fall of the Soviet Union's second empire.

Those scenes of joy must have seemed light years away to the people of Czechoslovakia only 20 years earlier. With the benefit of hindsight, and especially when Hungary's experience in 1956 is considered, Czechoslovak hopes of being allowed to build 'Communism with a human face' without Soviet intervention in 1968 seem painfully naive, but that ignores the genuine belief that the changes had been gradual and peaceful enough not to give the Soviet Union a reason to intervene.

Pressure for liberalization had been increasing both inside and outside the Communist Party for some months before Antonin Novotny was replaced as Party leader by Alexander Dubcek on 5 January 1968. What seemed to give cause for optimism when this change was made was that it appeared to have the Soviet Union's blessing. Novotny had fallen out of favor in Moscow, and Dubcek had established good connections with the USSR in his previous post of Party boss in Slovakia. However, the Soviet leadership was taken

people. The flow increased in 1960 and the first half of 1961.

On 13 August 1961 the Soviet sector of Berlin was sealed off by barricades. Suddenly it became impossible for residents of that sector and the rest of the GDR to travel into West Berlin without a special permit. No-one believed the excuse given by the East German authorities

aback at the pace with which reforms began. In March, the first criticisms of developments in Czechoslovakia were voiced by the Soviet Union and other East European countries. A number of senior personnel changes had already taken place, public rallies had been held to declare support for Dubcek's policies and the media was becoming more open. What must have been clear to the Kremlin even at this stage was that

Dubcek's reforms had already removed the essential element to keep the system stable: fear. People were beginning publicly to declare views for which they would have been imprisoned only a few months earlier. This was just the kind of 'disease' which Soviet leaders had feared might infect the rest of the empire when it appeared in Hungary in 1956.

In May, Dubcek and other Czechoslovak leaders were summoned to Moscow to be warned not to go too far. A number of senior Soviet Army officers visited Czechoslovakia, ostensibly in preparation for military exercises that the Soviets had persuaded the Czechoslovak leadership should take place on their territory in June. The first troops arrived on 30 May, although the exercises did not begin until 20 June. Ominously, the troops did not leave when the exercises ended. (Unlike Hungary, between 1945 and 1968 there were no Soviet forces stationed in Czechoslovakia.)

July saw further pressure put on the Czechoslovak leadership by 'the Warsaw Pact Five' (the USSR, GDR, Poland, Hungary and Bulgaria). Rumania took no part in this, having already shown signs of asserting its own 'independence.' Rumanian leader Nicolae Ceausescu's foreign policy did not always accord with the Kremlin's wishes: he maintained diplomatic relations with Israel after all the other Warsaw Pact members broke off relations during the Six-Day War in 1967; and he pursued, and established, relations with West Germany without the Soviet Union's approval. Domestically, Ceausescu established such a strict regime that Moscow

RIGHT: Young Czechs in Prague protesting to Soviet soldiers after the Warsaw Pact invasion of Czechoslovakia in August 1968. Many of the soldiers were bemused by the invasion, having been told either that they were on exercise in part of the Soviet Union, or that they were helping the Czechoslovaks.

was prepared to tolerate these gestures, since they represented no threat to the internal security of the empire.

The 'Five,' though, sent individual warning letters to the Czechoslovak leaders and then, on 15 July, made a joint declaration. In this, they denied any intention of planning to interfere in Czechoslovak internal affairs but, in the next breath, they said that they were not prepared to stand aside and let hostile forces tear Czechoslovakia away from the socialist community. Negotiations between the Czechoslovak and Soviet Communist Parties took place near the Czechoslovak-Soviet border from 29 July until 1 August. These seemed to give fresh hope that Czechoslovakia would be allowed to pursue its chosen path. What became clear later, though, was that the Soviet leaders were content to lull the Czechoslovaks into a false sense of security. Despite the smiles and the handshakes, when they returned to Moscow the Soviet leaders set in train concrete plans for the invasion to crush 'the Prague Spring.'

The invasion took place on the night of 20-21 August. It involved half a million men from the armies of the Warsaw Pact Five, though the majority of the troops were Soviet. As a military operation, it was a complete success; that vital ingredient, surprise, had been achieved totally.

But if it was a victory for the generals, it was a hollow one. The troops did not have to fight. There had been no armed uprising in Czechoslovakia, as there had been in Hungary 12 years earlier. The people of Czechoslovakia resigned themselves to their fate because, as it was later put 'you just can't go against tanks with bare hands.'

Politically, the invasion was an embarrassment for the Soviet Union. Unlike in Hungary, where after the invasion Janos Kadar readily agreed to form a government to the Kremlin's liking, in Czechoslovakia the Communist leadership stayed united behind Dubcek. It was impossible, therefore, for the Warsaw Pact members to talk of being 'invited in' to Czechoslovakia. The Soviet Union clearly decided that any criticism that it might suffer from the international community was worth it, since the prospects of Czechoslovakia leaving the socialist community and thus setting an example to its neighbors would have far more serious consequences. On 22 August, in an article to be dubbed in the West, 'the Brezhnev Doctrine' *Pravda* wrote that the defense of Czechoslovakia was an internationalist socialist duty. The message to the countries of the second empire was clear: the Soviet Union would be prepared to hold on to the empire at whatever cost.

ABOVE: A Soviet tank rumbles past a burning vehicle in Prague. On the whole, though, resistance to the Soviet-led invasion was light.

6
AN IMPERIALISTIC FOREIGN POLICY (1955-79)

LEFT: Symbol of a superpower: the Monument to the Space Conquerors in Moscow. It was a source of great Soviet pride that they beat the Americans into space.

In the Soviet Union's foreign policy, the second empire was always going to be the most important region for both strategic and ideological reasons. By the mid-1950s, however, the Soviet leadership was ready to start spreading its influence farther afield: the revolution was secure at home; and pro-Soviet regimes were firmly in place in Eastern Europe. The break-up of the former great colonial empires (such as the British, the French and the Portuguese) seemed to present an opportunity for developing two tenets of Marxism-Leninism: the Marxist one, which held that liberated nations would automatically spurn capitalism; and the Leninist one, which said that the proletariat would not achieve the revolution on its own and would need the guiding hand of the Communist Party.

In 1956, the aims of Soviet foreign policy were officially defined as follows:

1) To secure favorable conditions for the building of socialism.

2) To strengthen the unity and solidarity of the socialist countries.

3) To support national liberation movements and to cooperate with the developing countries.

4) To uphold the principle of peaceful coexistence of states with different social systems, to resist the forces of imperialism and to save mankind from a new world war.

Whilst these were the aims, the Soviet leadership were guided in their implementation by two key factors: relations with the United States of America and with China. These factors tempered the revolutionary enthusiasm inherent in the declared aims with an element of common sense. It also showed that the blind devotion to the cause which had inspired the Bolsheviks at

the time of the Russian revolution was long dead.

The position of the USA was vital to Soviet thinking for two reasons. Firstly, as the biggest and richest capitalist country in the world it was automatically the USSR's principal ideological enemy. Secondly, by exploding the atomic bombs at Hiroshima and Nagasaki to end World War II, the Americans had shown that their military power was a generation ahead of the Soviets'. The Soviet Union would have to obtain its own nuclear weapons and then persuade the rest of the world that it had caught up with America and was in a position to challenge the USA and the forces of capitalism worldwide.

Early in the 1950s the Soviet Union showed that it had succeeded in building a nuclear bomb, but technology had advanced. The great breakthrough with nuclear weapons was the harnessing of the nuclear explosive and the rocket. No longer would a country have to fly an aeroplane over enemy territory – with the inherent danger that the aircraft could be shot down – in order to deliver a nuclear attack. With a nuclear warhead fitted to a missile, an attack could be launched from a great distance. The next great advance in nuclear weapons was to be the introduction of multiple, independently-targetted warheads. One missile could have up to 10 warheads which, after the missile had done its initial job, could split away and hit different targets. By the time these were introduced in the 1970s, it was accepted that the USSR and the USA had parity in nuclear weapons systems.

The introduction of the nuclear missile meant that it was vital for the Soviet Union to show the world that it could compete with America. Two

BELOW: The Soviet leadership atop Lenin's mausoleum salute the Revolution Day Parade on Red Square, 1956. Nikita Khrushchev (center) was soon to establish himself as the undisputed ruler. But following such risky adventures as the Cuban Missile Crisis he was removed in a palace coup in 1964.

events in 1957, therefore, were crucial not only to the development of Soviet-American relations, but to the conduct of Soviet foreign policy over the next two decades. The first was the successful launch of a Soviet intercontinental ballistic missile. The second was the launch of the world's first space rocket, which carried a satellite into orbit in October 1957. The Soviet Union had now arrived on the world scene, and the advances in US technology had been wiped out – apparently. History was to reveal that there was a great deal of bluff in the Soviet stance, though this realization did not come in time to prevent the escalation of the arms race, through an American belief that the Soviets had caught up and a Soviet desire to close the real gap which they knew still existed.

Whereas the potential confrontation with the USA was because of the ideological struggle between capitalism and Communism, the Soviet dispute with China was over the right to be the leader of the world Communist movement. Relations between the Soviet Union and the Communist regime established in China by the revolution of 1949 were not deeply rooted. The Soviets had never given the Chinese Communists, led by Mao Tse-tung, their unequivocal support before the revolution. They chose to hedge their bets, in case Chiang Kai-shek's nationalists were successful. After the Chinese

Communist Party had taken power in 1949, its leaders never really forgave the Soviets for this.

Ostensibly, though, in the early 1950s the Soviet Union and China formed a great bastion of Communism, a supposed example to the rest of the world of the shape of things to come. However, the facade started to slip after the

ABOVE: A meeting of Warsaw Pact marshals.

BELOW: Heavy artillery in Red Square marking the Fortieth Anniversary of the Revolution, 1957.

RIGHT: Nikita Khrushchev with Chinese Communist Party leader Mao Tse-tung in 1958. The smiles were soon to fade, however, as relations between the two Communist giants soured.

Twentieth Congress of the Soviet Communist Party in 1956. The Soviets believed that the Chinese had accepted the ideas put forward at the congress on de-Stalinization, peaceful coexistence and the belief in a peaceful transition to socialism. Afterward however, the Chinese spoke out against what they saw as a watering-down of socialist values – revisionism, they called it. They claimed that this accounted for Yugoslavia's independent stance and, in the years that followed, it was to be an accusation that the Chinese leveled at the Soviet Union itself.

Although there were to be some changes of direction along the way, this was the essence of

RIGHT: Ever one for unorthodox behavior, Khrushchev holds an impromptu Press conference during his visit to the United Nations in New York in 1960. It was on this trip that he surprised many, and embarrassed others, by banging his shoe on the podium while addressing the UN.

Chinese criticism of Mikhail Gorbachev in the wake of the collapse of the Soviet Union. The Chinese leadership of the Eighties and Nineties claim that their method of allowing certain changes in economic policy whilst keeping a firm grip on the country – as epitomized by the way in which the pro-democracy demonstrations were dealt with in Tiananmen Square in June 1989 – was the correct way to allow a socialist society to adapt to the times without destroying socialism. In Soviet terms, the Chinese had economic *perestroika* (restructuring) without political *glasnost* (openness). The Chinese maintain that by introducing *glasnost* before *perestroika* Mr Gorbachev dug his own grave.

From the initial criticisms in 1956, the Sino-Soviet relationship quickly fell apart. In November 1957, at a gathering of Communist parties in Moscow to mark the fortieth anniversary of the Bolshevik Revolution, Mao described how the East wind was prevailing over the West, and spoke of the millions of socialists who would survive the nuclear holocaust which would destroy capitalism. Such an assertion horrified the Soviet leadership. Even in his more extreme moments, Nikita Khrushchev, who had taken over as party leader in September 1953 and had become undisputed leader of the country by 1958, stuck to the view that 'the nuclear weapon does not obey the laws of the class struggle.'

Despite this disagreement over the utility of nuclear weapons, Mao returned from Moscow with an agreement from the Soviets to provide China with an atomic bomb and the details of its manufacture. The Chinese then claimed that the USSR was using this agreement as a way of trying to put China under Soviet control. The culmination of this argument was that in June 1959 the Soviet Union revoked the agreement. Sino-Soviet relations were irrevocably damaged, and for the next 25 years all Soviet attempts to spread their influence worldwide had to take into account the position of China, the 'upstart nation' which was trying to take the role of leader of world Communism away from the world's first socialist state.

Although it was not the first focus of attempts to create an extended ideological empire, perhaps the most significant country where the Soviets extended their influence was Cuba. Ironically, it accelerated the development of what was to be called 'the superpower relationship,' since much of the Soviet Union's involvement with Cuba was caused by the negative attitude of the USA to this revolution on its own doorstep. When the Cuban revolution took place in January 1959, it was not a socialist revolution. Its leader, Fidel Castro, denied that he was a Communist, and set as one of his goals a desire to occupy a position between the USA and the USSR. Yet less than three years later, in Decem-

ber 1961, Castro was to declare: 'I am a Marxist-Leninist, and I shall be a Marxist-Leninist until the last day of my life.' Just how much Castro's change of heart was genuine is open to debate, but whether or not he had become a Communist he had certainly shown a deeply practical streak in declaring his support for the Soviet cause.

Castro had wanted to establish good relations with his powerful neighbor, the USA. But the more he alienated the Americans by his socialist-oriented domestic policies, the more the Soviet Union came to represent a possible guarantor of Cuban security, and the more attractive the proposition seemed to be to Moscow to have a foothold in the Caribbean. At first, this change came about in the economic sphere. Cuba's economy relied heavily on its exports of sugar. The United States hoped to exert pressure on Cuba by cutting its Cuban sugar quota, which it did in July 1960, but the Americans failed to appreciate that Soviet influence had already started to grow.

In February 1960 there had been the first visit to Cuba of a high-level Soviet delegation led by Deputy Prime Minister Anastas Mikoyan. Mikoyan had signed a trade and aid agreement,

ABOVE: Mao Tse-tung waves to crowds during a rally in Peking celebrating the Cultural Revolution in 1966. Mao is wearing the armband of the Red Guards, the often fanatical youngsters who sought to root out 'bourgeois' behavior among the Chinese people.

RIGHT: Fidel Castro addresses his troops and admirers during the revolution of January 1959. Castro initially denied that he was a Communist. But when he saw that he had the support of Moscow and the wrath of Washington, he placed Cuba firmly in the socialist camp.

BELOW: Castro and Khrushchev meet for the first time at the UN in September 1960.

which upped the amount of sugar the Soviet Union was to buy in return for Soviet merchandise and hard currency. When the Americans announced that they were cutting their imports of Cuban sugar, the Soviets stepped in and bought the 700,000 tons the Americans had cut. In October, Washington announced a complete economic embargo on Cuba. This meant that Cuba turned more firmly to Moscow, and began to look for military assurances, since Castro feared that, after the failure of their economic policy, the Americans might try to overthrow his regime by force.

Castro's fears were justified. In April 1961 a group of Cuban exiles, acting with American support, landed at the Bay of Pigs. This supposed 'invasion' was a farce, a poorly-planned operation which had no hope of success, but it did help to persuade the Kremlin that Castro needed protection, and by the end of the year the Soviet Union was supplying significant quantities of arms to Cuba. Now it was to be Khrushchev's turn to make a serious miscalculation – one so serious that it could have led to a third world war. In an enormous gamble, Khrushchev decided to install nuclear missiles in Cuba. This seems to have been less for Cuba's own protection than as a way of swiftly altering the strategic balance of power. Either way, it failed.

It seems that, as was to be the case with the invasion of Afghanistan 18 years later, the decision to send missiles to Cuba was taken without the knowledge of many senior members of the Soviet leadership. American intelligence was aware that plans were being made, as on 4 September 1962 the White House issued a statement saying that 'the gravest issues would arise' if offensive missiles were installed in Cuba. Four days later, a Soviet ship docked in Cuba carrying the first secret delivery of these weapons. What happened next was a triumph for US intelligence and diplomacy. On 14 October, the CIA presented President John F. Kennedy with incontrovertible photographic proof, taken by US spyplanes, that the Soviet Union was building nuclear missile sites in Cuba. Thanks to information received from an American spy in Moscow, the Americans were able to assess accurately what stage construction had reached, and estimate how long it would be before the sites would be operational. Thus, a pre-emptive strike by Washington, which would almost certainly have

brought a response from Moscow, was avoided.

On 22 October, President Kennedy addressed the American nation. He spoke of the presence of Soviet missiles in Cuba, announced that he was imposing a naval quarantine of all offensive military equipment to Cuba and declared that any nuclear missile launched from Cuba against any nation in the Western hemisphere would be regarded as an attack by the Soviet Union on the USA. Such an action would bring a full retaliatory response against the USSR. For six days, the world held its breath. At no time, before or since, did the superpowers come closer to all-out nuclear war. Then, after much frantic behind-the-scenes diplomatic activity, including 10 personal messages exchanged by Kennedy and Khrushchev, the Soviet leader announced on 28 October that a new order had been issued to dismantle the weapons. He also expressed his trust in Kennedy's assurance that no attack would be made on Cuba.

Castro was furious, since he felt that he had been used as a pawn in the superpowers' game. He had been persuaded to 'request' the missiles, although it seems that the whole initiative had been Khrushchev's; the missiles were wholly under Soviet control; and the final agreement

BELOW: Incontrovertible proof that the Soviet Union was trying to put nuclear missiles on Cuba. This photograph was one of a series taken by American spyplanes which led to the exposure of Khrushchev's plan before it could be completed.

ABOVE: In the wake of the Cuban Missile Crisis, President Kennedy tours US air defense stations in Florida.

had been reached without Castro being consulted at all. The Cuban Missile Crisis led to a major rift in Soviet-Cuban relations. While remaining trading partners – largely to Cuba's advantage – Castro was no longer prepared to toe Moscow's ideological line. Throughout the Sixties, Castro adopted an aggressive stance, calling openly for armed struggle in the Third World to bring about the revolution. This was embarrassing for Moscow, but a combination of

RIGHT: Friends again. His anger over the Missile Crisis having abated, Fidel Castro visits Moscow in January 1964. But he was to continue criticizing the Soviet Union for the next few years.

factors brought about a rapprochement toward the end of the decade.

The USSR used Cuba's dependence on Soviet oil and the new trade agreement due to be signed in 1968 to put pressure on Castro to modify his rhetoric. At the same time, the revolutionary movement in Latin America all but collapsed, most symbolically with the death of Che Guevara in 1967. With the possibility gone of other Latin American countries joining Castro's cause, he recognized the need for Moscow's continued protection. Soviet-Cuban relations were institutionalized in 1972, when Cuba became the first country of the 'overseas empire' to join the Communist trading bloc, Comecon. This brought Cuba more firmly under Moscow's influence and led to internal political changes, such as making Cuba's political system one of the Soviet, Marxist-Leninist type. Moscow could also use the added pressure of the other members to ensure that Castro would not pursue policies which did not fit in with its wishes.

Castro did not rock the boat, but it remains difficult to see what great advantages the Soviet Union obtained from its close relationship with Cuba: it did not serve as a model of socialist development for other Third World countries; it did not provide a military base from which the USA could be threatened; but it was to be a drain on Soviet resources. In the classic colonial empires, the flow of resources went the other way.

Useful though it was for the Soviet Union to have a foothold in the United States' backyard, the most important region for Soviet political and strategic expansion in the late Fifties and the Sixties was the Middle East. It was an area which had been dominated by Western powers, but where nationalist liberation movements were emerging. The deployment of the US Sixth Fleet in the Mediterranean was seen as a threat to Moscow's ability to deploy its own Black Sea Fleet which relied on free access through the Dardanelles. If the Caribbean was America's backyard, then the Middle East was the Soviet Union's, with only a few hundred miles separating the USSR's southern border from Cairo, Damascus, Baghdad and Riyadh.

Soviet involvement in the Middle East began in September 1955, when President Gamal Abd al-Nasser of Egypt signed a deal to buy arms

BELOW: A Soviet-Egyptian celebration to mark the eighth anniversary of the starting of the building of the Aswan Dam. This was the grandest project undertaken by the Soviet Union in the Middle East, but this and other gestures failed to win the support in the region which the USSR was aiming for.

from Czechoslovakia, following refusals by the West to help him modernize his army. Given Moscow's domination of Eastern Europe, the Czech arms deal gave the Soviet leadership the foot in the door that they needed to begin expanding their influence. The Soviet Union sealed its friendship with Egypt by financing the building of the Aswan Dam, a vital project for Egypt and an important, if expensive, symbol for the Kremlin that it was now a force to be reckoned with in the Middle East.

The Soviet Union continued to spend large sums of money to increase its importance in the area. By the mid-1960s Soviet delegations were welcome in Iraq, Syria, Yemen and Algeria, as well as Egypt. In June 1967 the Soviet Union was given the opportunity to extend its influence still further. It seems that the Soviet leadership was as surprised as the Arab world by the Israeli attack on Egypt, Jordan and Syria on 5 June 1967. In just six days, the Israelis took the Sinai peninsula, the West Bank of Jordan and the Golan Heights. Whilst some Arab voices blamed the swift defeat on a lack of Soviet support, the Kremlin was quick to move into the void left by the shock. If such a strike were not to be repeated, the Soviet leadership believed that a military presence would have to be established in the Middle East.

Military facilities were secured in Egypt, Syria, Iraq and Algeria. Thousands of military advisers

were sent to Egypt and Syria to try and rebuild those countries' shattered armies. The deployment of Soviet warships in the Mediterranean was greatly increased, and naval facilities were obtained in Egypt, Iraq, Somalia and Yemen. While all this was in progress, the Soviet Union concluded treaties of friendship and cooperation with Egypt (in 1971) and Iraq (in 1972). But all was not well with Soviet relations in the Middle East. Most importantly, relations began to sour with Egyptian President Anwar Sadat. In 1972 the Soviets turned down Sadat's request for large quantities of modern weapons. Sadat responded by expelling over 15,000 Soviet military experts and virtually cutting off relations. The outcome of the dispute showed which side put greater store by the relationship, as the USSR resumed arms supplies to Egypt in 1973.

However, this was to prove a temporary rapprochment. The next Arab-Israeli conflict, the Yom Kippur War of October 1973, saw more criticism of the Soviets by the Arabs, again for allegedly failing to provide them with the right equipment. The Soviets responded by accusing the Arabs – and Egypt in particular - of ingratitude, and of failing to realize that cooperation is a two-sided matter. It became more and more clear that Sadat wanted to develop closer relations with the Americans, and regarded the Soviets as a nuisance. Finally, in March 1976, he unilaterally abrogated the Soviet-Egyptian Treaty.

BELOW: Leonid Brezhnev and Egyptian President Gamal Abd al-Nassar face each other across the negotiating table in the Kremlin, July 1968. But relations with Egypt turned sour after Anwar Sadat, on Nasser's right, became president in 1970.

The extent to which Soviet influence in the Middle East collapsed after this can be seen by a passage in Leonid Brezhnev's speech as General Secretary to the Twenty-sixth Communist Party Congress in 1981. Twenty-six years after establishing a presence in the Middle East, during which time the Soviet Union counted as its friends in the region Egypt, Iraq, Syria, Algeria, Sudan, Ethiopia, Somalia and Yemen, Brezhnev chose to mention only Yemen as a country of 'socialist orientation.' An important reason for the Soviet Union's failure in the Middle East were the changes that took place within the countries of the region which altered the perspectives of those countries. The nationalistic fervor of the 1950s had become moderated 20 years later.

Leaders changed, too, most significantly in Egypt, where the Soviet Union realized too late how much more conservative and pro-Western Sadat was compared to Nasser. Furthermore, Soviet influence never extended to the largest and the richest country in the area, Saudi Arabia. In the Seventies and Eighties, Saudi Arabia gave financial aid to a number of its neighbors – and, indeed, countries farther afield, such as Afghan-

LEFT: President Sadat addressing his nation in October 1970. Sadat wanted better relations with America than with the USSR. After some years of tension, Sadat unilaterally abrogated the Soviet-Egyptian Treaty in 1976.

BELOW: Brezhnev playing host to West German Chancellor Willi Brandt on the Black Sea in 1971. Relations between the Soviet Union and West Germany were beginning to thaw. But any talk of German unification, which was to come 20 years later, was excluded.

istan, South Korea and Zaire – in order to combat what it saw as the Communist threat.

The specter – or the promise – of Communism was indeed an essential ingredient in Moscow's

RIGHT: The Soviet Union tried to extend its influence in Africa by sending weapons and surrogate troops to take part in the civil war in Angola. Here a Unita guerrilla holds a Soviet AK-47 rifle, while standing beneath a poster of the Unita leader, Jonas Savimbi.

BELOW: The beginning of detente. Brezhnev chats to US President Richard Nixon following the signing in the Kremlin of a number of agreements between the two countries, June 1974. US Secretary of State Henry Kissinger is in the foreground.

policy in the Middle East from the mid-Fifties to the late Seventies. This was less through a desire to establish Soviet-type political systems there, although that would have been a welcome bonus, rather the Soviet Union's main aim was to extend its influence to the detriment of the Western powers. In the end this policy failed, totally and expensively. The reason why was that in its analysis of the region the Kremlin was too tied up by its own ideology. The ideology led Soviet leaders to gloss over local differences based on religion, culture or even race, seeing the eventual 'class' goal of Marxism-Leninism as the driving factor. This was a mistake.

Elsewhere, the Soviet Union seemed less besotted with the idea of the 'inevitable' victory of Communism. In Africa, for example, it had been recognized by the late 1960s that post-colonial states were not embracing Communism with open arms. This was reflected in the drop in Soviet aid to African countries, especially sub-Saharan Africa: in the 10 years from 1954 to 1964, Africa received about 47 percent of all Soviet aid to the Third World; but in the next 10-year

period, to 1974, Africa's share was just 13 percent. This greater realism was shown in 1976 when, following the Portuguese withdrawal from Angola in November 1975, the Soviet Union did not use its own forces to help bring to power the Popular Movement for the Liberation of Angola, but surrogate troops from Cuba. This gave Moscow the chance to direct the overall strategy without making it too obvious.

The Soviet Union's attempts to spread the revolution between 1955 and 1979, therefore, could in no way be described as successful. It did manage to establish useful facilities around the world, such as friendly ports for Soviet merchant and naval vessels, but on the whole a vast amount of energy, resources and money was spent only to have many doors slammed in the Kremlin's face. Even in those countries where the Soviets remained welcome guests, such as Cuba, Vietnam and North Korea, it cost the USSR vast sums of money which could have been better spent back home, but the Soviet Union's ultimate foreign policy failure was to come right at the end of the 1970s.

7
THE LIMITS OF EMPIRE BUILDING

On 27 December 1979, Soviet troops entered Afghanistan. Little did they – or their political masters in the Kremlin – imagine that the adventure on which they were embarking would see the Soviet Army embroiled in a war which was to last more than twice as long as World War II. Nearly 15,000 Soviet soldiers and officers were to die in Afghanistan and over 50,000 others were to be wounded. A million Soviet citizens were to serve there, and all of them came away at least mentally scarred. Millions of others learnt that the version of events that they received from the Soviet media bore little relation to the harsh reality of what was actually going on in Afghanistan. The Afghan War was to have a profound effect on the Soviet mentality, and was a contributory factor to the social malaise which helped lead to the collapse of the system.

The history of the Soviet invasion of Afghanistan began in April 1978, when the People's Democratic Party of Afghanistan (PDPA) overthrew the existing regime of Mohammad Daoud Khan. The Soviet Union, which had had some 3000 advisers working in Afghanistan under Daoud, was the first country to grant diplomatic recognition, and began to give even greater help to the new regime. Soviet involvement increased with the signing of the Treaty of Friendship and Good Neighborliness in December 1978. Following the signature of the treaty, the number of

Soviets in the country rose to some 4500, of which about one-third were military advisers.

The first major threat to the new Afghan regime came in March 1979, when there was a popular uprising in the town of Herat. Resentment against Soviet involvement in Afghanistan, even at this early stage, was shown by the reaction of the rebels to 50 Soviet citizens in the town. Whilst other foreigners were left alone, or even protected, the Soviets were sought out, publicly tortured and killed. The revolt was crushed in five days, but it had serious repercussions both in Kabul and in Moscow. In a reorganization of the Afghan government, Foreign Minister Hafizullah Amin replaced Nur Mohammad Taraki as prime minister. Taraki stayed on, for the time being, as president and party leader.

Moscow reacted to the uprising by sending the head of the Soviet Army's Military-Political Directorate, General Aleksei Yepishev, on a fact-finding mission to Kabul. It is highly probable that on his return Yepishev briefed the Politburo on the possibility of Soviet military intervention. For the time being, the Soviet Union contented itself with stepping up its supplies of military equipment.

In October 1979, a terse announcement was made saying that Taraki – who had been at odds with Amin for some months – had died 'after a serious illness.' Amin, with whom Moscow's re-

BELOW: Soviet missile launchers situated near Kabul in January 1980. Soviet troops were told that they were going to Afghanistan to help the local population. Many were shocked to find that they were required to fight.

lations were far from good, was now in complete control. The Kremlin made dutiful noises about continuing to develop fraternal relations with Afghanistan but, with the country now in the grip of civil war, sent more military advisers. By the fall, Soviet officers were serving right down to company level in the Afghan Army.

Exactly when it was decided to send troops into Afghanistan is still unclear, although the final decision was probably taken in early to mid-December 1979. It was almost certainly made by a small group in the leadership: Party General Secretary Leonid Brezhnev, Defence Minister Marshal Dmitry Ustinov, Prime Minister Aleksei Kosygin, and Foreign Minister Andrei Gromyko. (After Mikhail Gorbachev became General Secretary in March 1985 – by which time all but Gromyko were dead – it was pointed out publicly that the decision had been so secret that 'even members of the Politburo did not know.' In December 1979, Gorbachev was the most recent addition to the Politburo, having been made a candidate (non-voting) member in November 1979.)

If the political decision to go into Afghanistan was highly controversial, the military execution of that decision was exemplary. From the middle of December some 1500 soldiers were flown into Kabul. Given the circumstances of the time – the war, the high number of Soviet advisers already

in the country – this did not arouse undue suspicion. They were followed on 24 December by a brigade (also about 1500 troops) from the 105th Airborne Division. In an operation reminiscent of the seizure of Prague in 1968, they took over

BELOW: Soviet Army vehicles arriving in Kabul in January 1980.

ABOVE: For some Soviet soldiers the war in Afghanistan was brief. Here Mujaheedin fighters sit atop a Soviet tank knocked out in fighting in January 1980.

vention in – Afghanistan in three ways. Firstly, the Soviet leadership claimed that there had been a request for assistance from the Afghan government. Secondly, they said that the USSR was obliged to give such assistance if requested under the terms of the 1978 Friendship Treaty. Thirdly, they maintained that the Soviet Union was simply helping Afghanistan to defend itself against foreign armed aggression in accordance with Article 51 of the United Nations' Charter.

The first of these reasons seems absurd. Even before he had taken over control in October 1979, Hafizullah Amin had persistently maintained that the Afghan Army alone would fight the opposition. Furthermore, since one of the first acts of the invasion was the assassination of Amin, it seems unlikely that he would have signed his own death warrant. Secondly, whilst the Friendship Treaty did include a clause on mutual military assistance, this reason for the invasion would have been valid only if there had been a genuine request for help. The final reason given was the most ridiculous, carrying as it did the implied threat that America was about to invade Afghanistan. As the Soviets well knew, America was preoccupied with events in Afghanistan's neighbor Iran, where the previous month Iranian fundamentalists had seized the US Embassy in Tehran, taking hostages.

If the Kremlin thought that America was too concerned with Iran to notice the invasion of Afghanistan, and that the rest of the Western world would start thinking about it only after the Christmas holidays, then it miscalculated. The West was outraged by the invasion. The process of detente, which had been so carefully built up throughout the Seventies, was dealt a severe blow. America introduced economic sanctions, refusing to sell grain to the Soviet Union. In fact, the Soviets found that other countries, notably Argentina and Canada, were prepared to step into the breach, and thus this became more of a moral stand by the USA than an effective action. Perhaps most significant of all, though, was the effect that the Afghan invasion had on the Olympic Games in Moscow in the summer of 1980. The USA led a boycott of the Games. Other countries, such as Britain, allowed their athletes to compete, but only under the Olympic, not their national, flag. This was a severe blow to Soviet pride. Sport was always seen as a vital weapon in the Soviet propaganda arsenal. The achievements of Soviet sportsmen and women were supposed to demonstrate to the world the advantages of the socialist system. The sports arena was a place where the confrontations upon which the Cold War was based could be fought out, but without the risk of death.

So to be denied the opportunity not only to compete with the Americans in the world's greatest sporting competition, but also in the one which was actually taking place in Moscow,

Kabul airport and key sites around the city. In the next three days a further 5000 military advisers arrived.

The final preparation was carried out on 26 December. After a failed attempt by Amin's Soviet cook in the Presidential Palace to poison him, a team of crack special forces, *Spetsnaz*, stormed the palace and killed Amin. Babrak Karmal, one of the leaders of the Parchami faction of the PDPA, who had been sent in virtual exile as ambassador to Prague following an internal party split in mid-1978, was flown in from Moscow and installed in power. On 27 December, the first columns of tanks and armored personnel carriers bearing 85,000 troops crossed into Afghanistan from Soviet Central Asia.

The Soviet Union attempted to justify the invasion of – or, as they described it, the inter-

hurt the Soviets deeply. The real reason why the Soviet Union boycotted the 1984 Olympics in Los Angeles was not because of fears for the safety of Soviet athletes, as Soviet officials claimed when they withdrew from the games, but a direct tit-for-tat response to the American boycott in 1980.

As the Afghan War gound on, misjudgements of how the rest of the world would react to the Soviet invasion became less important than the failure to assess properly the situation in the country or to devise a clear strategy for dealing with it. What soon became clear was that the Soviet invasion was not the first step in any grand expansionist plan aimed at Asia or the Middle East. In time, it also became obvious that the Soviet Army did not even intend to conquer

ABOVE: One of the problems that the Soviet Army had to adapt to in Afghanistan was the terrain. The Mujaheedin take to horseback in the Doab Valley, on their way to attack Soviet positions near Herat, January 1980.

LEFT: Soviet T-62 tanks on the move to Afghanistan.

RIGHT: The Afghanis —
both the Mujaheedin and
those on the government
side, as shown here —
had a bewildering array
of weapons. This group
show off a British-made
.303 Lee Enfield rifle of
World War I design, a
Soviet-made sub-
machine gun from World
War II, and a modern
Kalashnikov.

BELOW: Glad to be going
home. Soviet soldiers
among the first batch to
leave at the start of the
withdrawal of Soviet
forces, May 1988.

Afghanistan. There were large areas of the country where Soviet troops never set foot.

The intention in the somewhat befuddled minds of those who sent in the troops had been to give aid to ensure an element of stability in the region. It seems likely that, far from seeing the army as any kind of invading force, they intended it as a continuation of the policies which the Soviet Union had been pursuing since the PDPA had come to power in April 1978: military advisers were already helping the Afghan regime; here were a further 85,000 But it was the failure to establish a long-term goal for these 85,000 'military advisers' which led to the Soviet presence lasting for so long. A common complaint among senior officers by the mid-1980s was that the number of troops sent – which, at its peak, rose to 110,000 – was insufficient to perform what they saw as the army's task in Afghanistan. They believed that a massive force should have been sent in to wipe out all opposition to the regime, and that such a force would have been home within a matter of months, though given the difficult terrain and the skill of the guerrillas, this was unlikely.

On paper, such a suggestion sounded plausible, but in the mountains of Afghanistan, it is highly unlikely that such a strategy would have worked. At least, not if the Soviet Union was concerned about leaving any vestige of Afghanistan's infrastructure still intact for their friends in the Kabul government.

The Soviet media was obliged to write about the Soviet presence in Afghanistan in the most glowing terms. For the first two years or so, all talk of Soviet forces 'fighting' in Afghanistan was banned. When stories did begin to appear in the newspapers, in 1982 and 1983, any fighting in which the Soviet Army became involved was reported as being purely by chance, as the result of 'an ambush' whilst the unit was 'on exercise.' By

1983 it was no longer possible to hide completely the fact that Soviet soldiers were dying in Afghanistan. Too many families all over the USSR had received their sons back in sealed zinc coffins for this to be concealed totally, yet the majority of the population still gained the impression from the tightly-controlled media that the Soviet Army was carrying out an operation in Afghanistan akin to that of a UN peace-keeping force.

The web of deceit and lies which grew up around the Afghan War had a profound effect on Soviet psychology. People were used to the slogans of Communism which proclaimed that life was getting better, when many could see that it clearly was not. But the slogans of the Afghan War were different, because the lies covered up not economic failures, but the deaths of thousands of Soviet citizens, fighting for an unspecified cause in a hostile land. If you could lie about that, you could lie about anything. Small wonder, then, that when Mikhail Gorbachev blew the lid off many such secrets with his policy of *glasnost*, there was not only a great sense of wonder at the truth being available, but deep resentment, too.

Every cloud, they say, has a silver lining, and Poland can probably be grateful for the Soviet invasion of Afghanistan, because it stopped Soviet tanks from rolling there. The perceived threat to the future of socialism posed by the rise of the Solidarity trade union movement was so great that in December 1981 the Polish government declared martial law, largely to show Moscow that they were capable of sorting out their own problems.

The Soviet leadership would, in any case, have been reluctant to send troops into Poland after the sobering experience of sending the troops into Afghanistan. Given the way in which that move had soured international relations, what greater outcry would there be if the Soviet Army intervened in a European country? Given the lack of success against the Afghan mujaheedin guerrillas, how effective would the army be if thrown into a fight with a Polish Army determined to defend its country to the death?

Poland had already twice faced the threat of Soviet military intervention. The workers' demonstrations in Poznan in June 1956 were Poland's first concerted protests against the socialist regime and Soviet domination. The Polish authorities themselves managed to restore order then, although in the process over 50 people died and hundreds more were injured. Perhaps the Poles had saved themselves from a worse fate. Four months later, the Soviet Army showed the Hungarians that Moscow would not tolerate any deviations from what it perceived as the true path forward, with far greater casualties.

In December 1970, the Polish authorities again managed to quell unrest, after an announcement

ABOVE: The last Soviet troops leave Afghanistan.

of food price rises led to mass strikes and protests throughout the country. The trouble had started in the Baltic port of Gdansk, and it was here that the government showed that it would not tolerate such behavior by opening fire on the workers. In January 1971, strikes broke out again. The new leader, Edward Gierek, who had replaced Wladyslaw Gomulka after the trouble in December, took a huge risk for a Communist leader. He traveled to Gdansk and appealed directly to the workers for their cooperation. No doubt because they were amazed that their

LEFT: 15 February, 1989: Lieutenant-General Boris Gromov, the last commander of the Soviet forces in Afghanistan, gets back into his armored personnel carrier and waves a final farewell to the country. General Gromov was the last combat soldier to leave Afghanistan, and symbolically walked the last hundred meters across the border.

leader should actually try to reason with them, rather than simply employ strong-arm tactics, the Gdansk shipyard workers agreed to cooperate. In return, they were promised that the party would never lose touch with them again, and Gierek announced the start of Poland's 'Great Leap Forward.'

For the first couple of years, this brought genuine rewards, as national income rose impressively and more goods became available, but the early Seventies were to prove a false dawn for the new Poland. The recession in the West which followed the oil crisis of 1973 pushed up the price of imports and cut the demand for Polish exports. The country's foreign debt rose dramatically and shortages became a part of everyday life. Trouble broke out again in 1976, once more sparked off by an announcement of price rises for food. The headquarters of the Polish United Workers' Party (PZPR) in the town of Radom was ransacked, and in the ensuing riot four people died. The government was so frightened that the price rises were abandoned that same day, but the authorities fought back in other ways, firing strikers and arresting their leaders.

The first organized opposition group now appeared: the Committee for the Defense of the Workers (KOR). Although its aim was to provide money and legal aid to workers who had been arrested following the troubles in June 1976, in a one-party state where such an activity inevitably went against the wishes of the party, KOR became virtually a political organization. In September 1977, KOR began an underground newssheet, called *Robotnik* (*The Worker*).

KOR's success inspired others to publish newspapers and even arrange political meetings. But rather than employing the full machinery of the state against these opponents, Gierek simply relied on a series of police raids to frighten them into submission. Police would break up meetings and, with the aid of specially recruited thugs, beat up the participants. This approach, however, merely made people even more determined in their opposition to the regime.

Poland had a particular factor which caused problems for the Communist authorities, in that

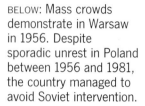

BELOW: Mass crowds demonstrate in Warsaw in 1956. Despite sporadic unrest in Poland between 1956 and 1981, the country managed to avoid Soviet intervention.

it had long been, and remained, a profoundly Catholic country. Although this did not sit comfortably with the official atheistic ideology, even the Kremlin was sensitive enough to realize that it would have been highly dangerous to make a concerted attack on the Church in the way that the Communists had done in Russia in the wake of the 1917 revolution. In 1977, the Church began to cooperate informally with the opposition, and in many rural areas the local priest was often the opposition leader.

The importance of the Church in Poland was underlined in October 1978, when a Pole, Cardinal Karol Wojtyla, was chosen to be the new Pope. To many Poles this was nothing short of a miracle, even a sign from God that he had not forgotten them. This feeling was heightened in May 1979, when Pope John Paul II, as the Polish Pope had become, made a nine-day pilgrimage to his homeland. Without being so tactless as to come out with open criticism of the regime, the Pope inspired people to strive for the greater good of Poland. The combination of a strong Church, and a Pole as its world leader, was to give the Polish opposition renewed strength in the struggles which were fast approaching.

By the end of the 1970s, the Polish economy was in a dreadful state: 'The Great Leap Forward' had fallen flat on its face; there was massive foreign debt and food shortages; and the consumer goods that Poles had been tempted by just a few years earlier had all but disappeared. Gierek continued to maintain that the party was still following the correct path; it was the government which had got it wrong. This distinction was absurd in a Communist country, since the government was effectively a rubber stamp for the party's policies. As a sop, Prime Minister Piotr Jaroszewicz was forced to resign, to be replaced by Edward Babiuch.

But Babiuch's government was soon antagonizing the population in much the same way as its predecessors. On 1 July 1980, price rises, modest in scale, but significant, were announced. Strikes broke out spontaneously all over the country. Gierek remained inactive. Indeed, given his earlier indecisiveness, it is difficult to see what he could effectively have done now, but his problems were set to intensify. On 14 August the workers in the Lenin shipyard in Gdansk, the main cause of the troubles in 1970, went on strike, demanding the reinstatement of a worker sacked for being a political activist. The cause was taken up by one of the leaders of the 1970 strike, who had been sacked in the political crackdown of 1976: Lech Walesa.

Remembering 1970, Gierek knew that this strike would take more to settle than an agreement on extra pay. The government entered into direct negotiations with the strikers, but by the time that they had signed the Gdansk Agreement on 31 August, the government was not

dealing simply with a strike committee. They were dealing with the 'independent, self-managing trade union' Solidarity. Solidarity was a trade union, not a political party. There was even an understanding that the PZPR could continue to rule, provided that it take more notice of the people. In the circumstances, such idealized visions could not hope to succeed. The fact that Solidarity, from its inception, stood up to the party and won suggested that here was a genuine opposition movement, and in any case, the PZPR had already shown its incompetence in running the country. Even changing leaders again, as happened in September 1980 when

ABOVE: Striking workers outside the Lenin shipyards in Gdansk in August 1980. The Lenin shipyards were the birthplace of Solidarity (whose logo can be seen at the top of the picture), and it was here that Solidarity's leader, and Poland's first post-Communist President, Lech Walesa, worked.

ABOVE: Lech Walesa is carried shoulder high as Solidarity supporters celebrate.

BELOW: Pope John Paul II after the assassination attempt, 13 May 1981.

the Polish borders with the USSR, Czechoslovakia and East Germany in December. These moves may have been real preparations for a Soviet invasion of Poland, or possibly just the Kremlin flexing its military muscles to reassure its neighbors and, at the same time, remind Poland of its obligations to the socialist community. Certainly, NATO took them to be genuine enough, as it issued official warnings to Moscow not to intervene. On 5 December, Warsaw Pact leaders held an emergency meeting in Moscow to discuss the Polish situation. The harshest criticism came from East Germany, but when the summit was over, the troops camped on Poland's borders stayed where they were. When they did move, it was back to base.

Poland breathed a sigh of relief, and went ahead with the week of commemoration to mark the tenth anniversary of the killing of the shipyard workers in Gdansk in 1970. The highlight of this came on 16 December, with the dedication of the 140-foot high steel monument to 'the Gdansk martyrs.' Uncomfortable though they must have felt, government and party leaders stood alongside the men's former colleagues, now Solidarity activists. Just how awkward this apparent reconciliation was, was shown in the new year. In January 1981, the government announced that it would be unable to fulfil that part of the Gdansk Agreement which said that all Saturday working must end. Once again, there were strikes throughout the country, ended only by a compromise agreement which gave the workers three Saturdays off out of every four.

The confrontational tone which was to typify 1981 had been set. In an ominous move, on 9 February General Wojciech Jaruzelski added the post of prime minister to that of defense minister. Though unconnected with the struggle between Solidarity and the government, May brought two events which seemed to cast a shadow over the immediate future. On 13 May, a Turk, Ali Agca, shot and seriously wounded the Pope in Rome, and two weeks later, the Primate of Poland, Cardinal Stefan Wyszynski, died.

Despite major personnel changes in the Central Committee and the Politburo of the PZPR at its congress in July, the new members proved no more ready or willing to effect real change than their predecessors had been. By the end of the summer, Solidarity had decided that it was a waste of time to put their trust in the existing authorities. From being merely a trade union trying to guarantee workers' rights, Solidarity now began to draw up plans for overt political activity.

Solidarity held its first congress in September and October 1981. Although far from living up to its name in the debates and discussions which raged at the congress, the overriding desire was quite clearly one for action. When proceedings were over, the congress issued an appeal to the

Gierek was dumped and Stanislaw Kania became first secretary in his place, was not now going to restore the party's credibility.

Developments in Poland were watched in horror by the other leaderships of Eastern Europe. Following loud criticism from Poland's neighbors, there were Soviet troop movements near workers of the Soviet Union and Eastern Europe to follow Solidarity's example, which brought a scathing reply from the Soviet news agency TASS, accusing Solidarity of being manipulated by Western secret services. It was the sort of language which had been heard about Czechoslovakia before the Soviet invasion in 1968.

In October, General Jaruzelski added to his powers by taking over the post of party first secretary from Stanislaw Kania. It was now, when he had so much power in his hands, that Jaruzelski began planning the military takeover. Relations between Solidarity and the authorities deteriorated still further, and, following a meeting of Solidarity's leaders in Gdansk on 11 December, the call went up for a day of national protest on 17 December.

The 17th – at least, that 17th which Solidarity had had in mind – never arrived. On the night of 12-13 December, Jaruzelski moved. Solidarity's buildings were seized and its leaders arrested. Telecommunications links with the outside world were cut off, and a curfew was imposed. The operation was stunningly successful. What was less successful was the way in which the military government then ran the country. It failed to bring in the sweeping changes that were so desperately needed in the economy, and it incurred the outrage of the West. Economic and political sanctions were imposed on Poland, adding to the country's woes. The situation remained grim even after martial law was lifted in July 1983.

The imposition of martial law failed to solve Poland's economic, political or social problems, but it did have one notable achievement. It removed the threat of Soviet military intervention.

Chastened by the experience of Afghanistan, the Soviet Union did not want to intervene in Poland. However, its leaders knew that they could not afford to have a breakaway country at the heart of the socialist empire, with the danger that its anti-socialist message could infect the other states. The more Solidarity became a political party, rather than a trade union, the greater would have been the risk of Soviet intervention. General Jaruzelski put a stop to that, but there were also developments back in the USSR itself which meant that foreign affairs were not at the top of the political agenda.

LEFT: Crowds in Warsaw begin to disperse after a two-hour warning strike in August 1981. Such social discontent made many, including Jaruzelski, believe that if the Poles did not put their own house in order, the Warsaw Pact armies would do it for them. By December, Jaruzelski saw martial law as the only option left open to him.

8
AT THE CROSSROADS

LEFT: Nikita Khrushchev haranguing the United
Nations during his visit in 1960.

Nikita Khrushchev was ousted from power in October 1964 because, great son of the working class though he was, he showed himself to be too spontaneous and too unpredictable in his behavior with regard to both foreign and domestic policy. However much they tried to put a brave face on it, the Soviet leadership knew that the Cuban Missile Crisis had been a debacle for the USSR. When Khrushchev banged his shoe on the rostrum at the United Nations, it was perceived as the action of a peasant, not a world statesman.

At home, Khrushchev had been so goaded by the Americans' claim (during his official visit in 1961) that they could grow better corn than the Russians, that he had devoted thousands of acres of arable land to growing corn which the Russians did not need. Furthermore, he proclaimed the rapid approach of Communism; but life continued as before. Thus, Khrushchev was to obtain a unique place in Soviet history: he was the only Soviet leader to be removed in a 'palace coup.' All other Soviet leaders until Mikhail Gorbachev died in office. Gorbachev ceased to be Soviet leader because the Soviet Union ceased to exist.

The rapid changes of Soviet leaders in the early 1980s – Brezhnev was in power until November 1982, then Andropov ruled for 15 months, before Chernenko took over in February 1984 – gave rise to the myth that Soviet leaders were always old. In fact, when Brezhnev became General Secretary in 1964 he was only 57 years old.

The crucial factor of the Brezhnev era was that he and his colleagues failed to take into account the way in which the world around them was changing. The more sympathetic view holds that this was because they did not appreciate that in those 18 years the world was not developing according to Marxist-Leninist norms. The more cynical view is that, although they realized that this was the case, the leadership was quite happy to trumpet the supposed achievements of socialism, as long as it brought personal benefits for them and those around them.

There can be no doubt that between 1964 and the late 1970s the lot of the average Soviet citizen improved considerably, but living standards in general still lagged way behind those of the West. The more the Seventies progressed, the more the country became bogged down in what was to be called in the Gorbachev era 'stagnation.' The Soviet economy still worked according to a virtual wartime principle: the military-industrial complex dominated everything, and central-planning ensured that the Soviet Army had everything it wanted, but the average consumer went without.

BELOW: Khrushchev holds an impromptu Press conference on the steps of the Lincoln Memorial in Washington. Although Krushchev's working class background made him an ideal candidate for Party leader, by the Sixties his colleagues realized that more sophisticated behavior was called for on the world stage.

Herein lay a crucial difference between the Soviet and Western economies. In the West, where the military was not the main consumer, there was a spin-off from technological developments into both the military and civilian sectors. (A simple, but vivid, example is velcro fastening. Originally designed for astronauts' space suits, it was quickly recognized that it could be put to good use in more down-to-earth ways.) In Brezhnev's Soviet Union, such spin-offs simply did not happen. The military got what the military wanted; the civilian economy tried to pick up any scraps which happened to fall from the rich Army's table. Largely as a result of this, by the late Seventies living standards had stopped rising, even if the Communist slogans continued to preach the inevitable triumph of socialism over capitalism.

Problems in the economy were exacerbated by the fact that, by the start of the 1980s, the Soviet leadership had become old – and it was beginning to show. When Leonid Brezhnev opened the Olympic Games in Moscow in 1980, he was looking frail; soon afterward there began a round of guessing games about the leader's health. The speculation was to continue on and off for two years, until Brezhnev died in November 1982. Whenever he failed to appear at an important function, the official line was always that General Secretary Brezhnev has 'a cold,' no matter how absurd and transparent this excuse grew to be. Such was the secrecy of the workings of the Kremlin, yet so greatly did Soviet leaders apply protocol, that over the years observers of Soviet politics – 'Kremlinologists' or 'Sovietologists' – learnt to assess the mood of the leadership, and the status of the individual leaders in tiny ways.

For example, the annual Red Square parade on 7 November to celebrate the anniversary of the Revolution was always eagerly awaited by Kremlinologists. This was partly to see what, if any, new military equipment would be put on show; but of more interest was the order in which the Party's Politburo lined up to review the parade on the top of Lenin's mausoleum. Whoever stood closer to the General Secretary was assumed to be in favor, while the absence of a Politburo member meant either a serious illness or a fall from grace.

One such occasion was the Kremlin gathering on the eve of the anniversary of Lenin's birth on 22 April. The man chosen to deliver the speech exhorting the party faithful to continue to do everything in Lenin's way was clearly someone who was well placed in the leadership. Also, however pressing were the affairs of state, any Politburo member flying abroad had to be accompanied to the airport by a team of his colleagues. The number of those in the delegation,

BELOW: Two months before his fall from grace in October 1964, Khrushchev toured farmlands in Kazakhstan. Some of his plans for Soviet agriculture, which were considered by his colleagues in the leadership to be harebrained, contributed to his downfall.

and who led it, said much about the significance of the departing member.

Such practices were to be highly significant in the first half of the 1980s. When Brezhnev flew to the Uzbek capital, Tashkent, in March 1982, the alarm bells rang when his return to Moscow was not shown on Soviet television. He had, in fact, had a stroke, though this was not announced, but as his demise approached, Brezhnev gave some signs himself that he was rapidly deteriorating. In September 1982 he went to Baku, the capital of Azerbaijan. Apart from it being obvious that he was having great difficulty in walking or talking at all, he made one memorably ironic blunder by saying how glad he was to be in 'Afghanistan,' not 'Azerbaijan.' (This was, of course, carefully edited out of all subsequent official texts.)

By November 1982, the charade could no longer be maintained. Brezhnev was clearly very ill when he appeared on the mausoleum for the parade. Three days later, on the evening of 10 November, Soviet television and radio began to prepare the population for the great shock of the announcement of the leader's death. A pop concert and an ice hockey match were dropped from the schedules, and a serious film about the life of Lenin shown instead. Moscow Radio began to play solemn music. These signs could mean only that a Soviet leader had died. The Kremlinologists began to speculate as to who it might be. Only during the next morning was the announcement made that it was Brezhnev, who had died at 8.30am on the 10th – 24 hours earlier.

Although it was nearly 30 years since a Soviet leader had died in office – Stalin in March 1953 – the sign now to watch for was: who had been made head of the funeral commission? When it was announced that this was to be Yury Andropov, people began to realize that Brezhnev's death might be of great significance after all.

Until May 1982, Andropov had spent 17 years as head of the Committee for State Security, the KGB. This was a time when the KGB had shown the Soviet population in no uncertain terms that any deviance from the official line would not be tolerated. While by no means on a par with Stalin's terror in the Thirties – execution for the

RIGHT: Leonid Brezhnev, General Secretary of the Communist Party, conferring with Konstantin Chernenko. Chernenko was largely thought to be Brezhnev's chosen successor. Having been beaten by Yury Andropov in the leadership selection after Brezhnev's death, Chernenko made a remarkable comeback to take over after Andropov's death 15 months later. But his year in office merely served to underline how decrepit the leadership had become.

political 'crime' of disagreeing with the regime no longer happened – Andropov led a determined crackdown on dissidents.

There were a number of 'celebrity' examples to act as warnings to the population at large. Perhaps the most famous was Alexander Solzhenitsyn; he had spent eight years in labor camps under Stalin and was determined that the world should know the extent of the horrors perpetrated there. In 1962, during the relaxation of censorship as part of Nikita Khrushchev's policy of de-Stalinization, Solzhenitsyn had been allowed to publish his fictionalized account of life in the camps, *One Day in the Life of Ivan Denisovich*, but after Khrushchev was ousted in October 1964, the thaw ended. Solzhenitsyn, however, refused to remain silent. The culmination of this came in February 1974, when the writer was expelled from the USSR and deprived of his citizenship, for 'anti-Soviet activities.'

Another man who felt the wrath of Andropov's KGB was Andrei Sakharov. Unlike Solzhenitsyn, Sakharov had been a highly honored son of the Soviet Union: a nuclear physicist, he had been called 'the father of the Soviet atom bomb.' Given the importance to the USSR of catching up with the Americans after the dropping of the atom bombs at the end of World War II, it would be impossible to underestimate the status this accorded. Sakharov had upset his masters, for as well as expressing regrets about his earlier work, he began to champion the cause of human rights.

LEFT: Yury Andropov in June 1983, during his 15-month spell as Party General Secretary and Soviet leader. Although the Kremlin tried to portray Andropov as an understanding and cultured man, he had been involved in some of the Soviet Union's most extreme repressions of the postwar period. He was Soviet ambassador in Hungary when Soviet troops went in to crush the uprising in 1956; then he was head of the KGB from 1967 to 1982.

In each of its revisions, the Soviet Constitution allegedly guaranteed full human rights to all its citizens. In practice, anyone who actively went against the official ideology by espousing different political views, or by actively proclaiming religious beliefs, risked imprisonment. When Andropov headed the KGB, this took on a new

LEFT: One man who felt the full force of Andropov's KGB was the writer Alexander Solzhenitsyn. Having suffered in Stalin's labor camps, Solzhenitsyn was hounded by the KGB for his writings which revealed the horrors perpetrated by the Soviet system. In February 1974 he was expelled from the USSR. The picture was taken when he received an honorary degree from Harvard University in June 1978.

interpretation, one that even Stalin had not thought of. Soviet logic went as follows: in Marxism-Leninism, the Communist Party has found the answer to all mankind's problems. There is no need, therefore, for other political parties, or even differing views, because if Marxism-Leninism is right in everything, then these other views must be wrong.

This, of course, had applied throughout Soviet history, but the appalling aspect which was added when Brezhnev led the Soviet Union and Andropov the KGB was the idea that, if you actively opposed the all-seeing, all-knowing party, not only were you wrong but you must be mad to think this way. The place for mad people was a psychiatric hospital, where they could be 'cured' with mind-numbing drugs. It was against such abuses that Sakharov spoke out. He paid for it firstly by being hounded by the KGB wherever he went, but it was the invasion of Afghanistan which was to be the final straw. Sakharov's was the lone voice which spoke out against the invasion in its first few days, at a time when many Soviet citizens were still blissfully ignorant of what had happened, so great was the official control over the media. To put him out of the reach of Western journalists, Sakharov was sent into internal exile in Gorky (now given back its old name of Nizhny Novgorod). Like many towns, cities and whole regions the length and breadth of the USSR, Gorky was closed to

foreigners. For seven years, Sakharov's protests were to be muted, though never completely stopped.

When Andropov took over as Soviet leader in November 1982, he behaved like a man who seemed to be aware that much needed to be done to change society, but that he might not have much time in which to do it. He was right on both counts. Almost immediately after taking over, he initiated changes both at the top and at the grass roots of Soviet life. In December, he moved Vitaly Fedorchuk – who had taken over when Andropov left the KGB in May – to head the Interior Ministry. Another of his former deputies, Viktor Chebrikov, took over at the top of the KGB. In this way, Andropov ensured that he was effectively in control of the two organizations which, in turn, controlled the population.

This intention to shake society out of the lethargy which had become the hallmark of the later Brezhnev years was seen on the ground by the establishment of the 'People's Control.' Officials accompanied by militiamen (police) would 'raid' shops, cinemas or parks during working hours questioning citizens as to why they were there when they should be at work. Many – at least in the shops – simply replied that if they did not spend hours going round the shops, their families would go hungry.

This not only confirmed to Andropov how bad things had got, but also showed him that many

BELOW: Andrei Sakharov was another famous dissident who suffered at the hands of Andropov's KGB, when the former nuclear scientist began to champion the cause of human rights. He was exiled to the city of Gorky, which was closed to foreigners, in January 1980, and only able to return to Moscow after a personal invitation from Mikhail Gorbachev in December 1986.

ordinary Soviet citizens had lost their respect for authority. Millions of people who were not interested in playing an active role in politics, and were not involved in high-level corruption, had become indifferent to the way the system was run, because they knew that not even Andropov could lock them all up – there would be no work force left! This did not mean that all these people were potential revolutionaries; far from it. The apathetic do not start revolutions. What it meant was that they would do no more than the minimum to improve society. Things had stagnated so much under Brezhnev that the Soviet Union needed a lot more than the minimum.

For all his understanding of what needed to be done, time was not on Yury Andropov's side. His health was beginning to fail by the spring of 1983, just a few months after he had taken over. Once again, the Kremlinologists began to look for tell-tale signs of who was in favor, to see who might replace Andropov if he were to die soon. Of the older generation, it was felt that the man many had tipped to replace Brezhnev – Konstantin Chernenko – was now out of the reckoning. People rarely had a second chance to impress in Soviet politics.

It was beginning to look more likely that the leadership would pass to the younger generation. Mikhail Gorbachev was already a clear contender. Having come into the Politburo as a candidate member in November 1979, he was made a full member the following year. He appeared to have great energy, as well as the backing of Andropov himself. In May 1983, Gorbachev was given the chance to make his first impression on the West, when he led a delegation to Canada. The West took note that this was clearly a new breed of Soviet leader.

Gorbachev was not the only younger man waiting in the wings, though. In May 1983, Grigory Romanov was moved to Moscow from his position as head of the party organization in Leningrad, to take up a powerful post as one of the Central Committee secretaries. Romanov was known as a hardliner, with strong connections in the military-industrial complex. Romanov also had weaknesses which were to be exploited in the near future. His surname counted against him, since it was the same as the last royal family, and jokes about putting another Romanov on the throne made some Soviet leaders decidedly uncomfortable. More significant was Romanov's expansive lifestyle. This was well illustrated by the story that at his daughter's wedding reception – held in the former czarist residence, the Winter Palace – a priceless dinner service which had belonged to Catherine the Great was smashed. Although the story was undoubtedly put about in order to discredit Romanov, it did raise doubts in many people's minds about his suitability to lead the country.

Domestically, Andropov's main achievement was to highlight the need for reform, although in the short time he was leader he actually achieved very little. In foreign policy his stated aim of improving relations with the USA was shattered by an event outside his control while he was on holiday in September 1983. In the early hours of 1 September, Korean Air Lines flight 007, flying from New York to Seoul via Anchorage, Alaska, was shot down while 700kms off course, and crossing Soviet airspace over the Far Eastern Kamchatka peninsula. The decision to shoot the plane down was taken at the local level, applying to the letter standing orders to Soviet air defense troops about how to deal with violations of the USSR's borders. At no time was the pilot who shot it down asked to comment on what he could see. Ground control having tracked the plane on radar, the pilot – an experienced major – was told to go and find 'the target.' Having found it and followed it, the order came from the

ABOVE: The pretender to the throne. Grigory Romanov, Leningrad Party boss, was thought to be Gorbachev's closest rival for the post of General Secretary in March 1985. But it was later revealed that his extravagant lifestyle and close association with certain elements of the old guard had already ruined his candidature by the time Chernenko died. He was also not helped by his surname, since it was the same as the last czarist dynasty.

RIGHT: West German
teenager Matthias Rust
lands his Cessna light
aircraft on Red Square in
May 1987. Although
there were great
suspicions that Rust had
been put up to the flight
by Western intelligence,
Gorbachev was swift to
use the incident to make
major changes in his
military high command,
including appointing
General (later Marshal)
Dmitry Yazov as Defense
Minister.

ground to shoot it down. He carried out his mission without question.

For some days, Moscow refused to admit that the Soviet Union had played any part in the downing of the aircraft. When an announcement was finally made, it was in the aggressive manner typical of Soviet propaganda, accusing the Americans of being responsible, because, they claimed, they were using a civilian aircraft for espionage purposes. However, the embarrassment of the political leadership showed through: six days after the incident, the Soviet armed forces' Chief of Staff, Marshal Nikolai Ogarkov, was forced into an unusually high profile position

to explain the shooting down at a Press conference. He, too, took the approach of attack, laying the blame at America's door.

The fact that the Soviets could not bring themselves even to apologize to the relatives of the 269 people who died reflected an underlying element of insecurity in the Soviet system. They were afraid to admit to having any weaknesses, even when they had been displayed for all the world to see. Any doubts as to the chaotic state of Soviet air defenses were dispelled three years later, when the young German Matthias Rust landed his Cessna light aircraft in Red Square in the middle of Moscow.

The Korean airliner incident put paid to any hope which Andropov had of improving superpower relations. Six weeks later, the dreaded Kremlin 'cold' struck; the Soviet leader was forced to cancel a trip to Bulgaria. On 7 November, he failed to appear on the mausoleum. Andropov lived on, in his hospital bed, until 9 February. His passing was even more melodramatic than Brezhnev's. On 9 February solemn music began on Radio Moscow but his death was not announced until the 11th.

This delay was because of the uncertainty which now plagued the leadership. While the Kremlinologists had been bracing themselves for the expected battle between Gorbachev and Romanov, Konstantin Chernenko had been rallying support among his colleagues. There were enough of them who could not bear to see the reins of power pass from their generation, and,

five days after Andropov's death, Chernenko was made the new General Secretary.

The 13 months that Chernenko was in power represented a vacuum in Soviet politics. The man was chronically ill with emphysema even before he took over. He was a grey, uninspiring figure, and the attempts to bolster his personality by tales of his service in the frontier guards on the Chinese border merely added to the impression that he was a nonentity. His presence was an embarrassment to the Soviet people, as he stumbled through his public appearances, shuffling rather than walking and losing his place in his speeches. Yet, ironically, Chernenko's infirmity actually helped Gorbachev, because it became abundantly clear to all that, after two-and-a-half years spanned by Brezhnev, Andropov and Chernenko, the gerontocracy's days leading the Soviet Union were over.

BELOW: British tabloid newspapers give their reaction to the shooting down of Korean airliner flight 007 by Soviet air defense fighters on 1 September 1983. In typical defensive style, the Soviet political and military leaderships blamed the act on US aggression, claiming that the Americans had been using a civilian airliner for espionage purposes.

9
THE NEW EMPEROR

LEFT: Mikhail Gorbachev, who became Soviet
leader in March 1985. Though a great
reformer, he was eventually to preside over the
break-up of the Soviet Union in 1991.

By late 1984, with Chernenko's health in obvious decline, Mikhail Gorbachev was looking ever more like the heir apparent. It became known that in the General Secretary's absence, it was Gorbachev who was hosting Politburo meetings. In December Gorbachev had the opportunity of presenting himself to the West as a new type of Soviet leader, when he made an official visit to Britain. The British Prime Minister, Margaret Thatcher, made it quite clear not only that the difference was recognized, but that she whole-heartily approved, when she declared: 'I like Mr Gorbachev; I can do business with him.'

Back home, in early 1985, there was a small but significant shift in the posturing of the Polit-buro. Grigory Romanov, considered by many to be Gorbachev's main rival for the leadership when Chernenko went, was being sidelined. When he realized he had lost his chance, Roma-nov threw his support behind Viktor Grishin, veteran head of the Moscow Party organization, and one of the last members of the old guard who stood any chance of hanging on to the reins of power for his generation. But when the denoue-ment came, Gorbachev proved unstoppable. A crucial factor was the support of the long-serv-ing Foreign Minister, Andrei Gromyko. Timing was also important: Chernenko died on 10 March, the official announcement was made the following morning, and that same afternoon came the news that Mikhail Sergeyevich Gor-

bachev was the new General Secretary. Never before had a Soviet succession been so quick.

Gorbachev knew that he had to move swiftly to stop the old guard from organizing. A crucial absentee at the Central Committee meeting which elected him on 11 March was Vladimir Shcherbitsky, the reactionary party boss in Ukraine. He was on an official visit to the USA and could not return in time. His belated return to Moscow was almost symbolic of the way in which the older generation had now been left behind.

Gorbachev began his 'reign' in similar fashion to Andropov: so much to do and so little time in which to do it. If society was sick in November 1982, then by March 1985 the illness had become chronic. The difference was that Gorbachev at least had the health and the energy to try and see it through. One of the first examples of the new style was shown when Gorbachev visited Lenin-grad in May 1985. Never before had the Soviet public been made privy to such open criticism of the Party machine, as was heard – and published – then. Gorbachev had an ulterior motive: he wanted to show up the corruption of the Lenin-grad party apparatus in order to hammer the final nail into the political coffin of his rival, Romanov.

He also showed a willingness previously un-known from leaders in the USSR to meet the people. In the first of many such displays, he went on a walkabout in Leningrad, shaking

BELOW: Burying the old guard. When Konstantin Chernenko died in March 1985, it meant that for the third time in two and a half years, a Soviet leader was laid to rest in the Kremlin Wall. Gorbachev, immediately on the left behind the coffin, would soon ensure that the Soviet Union would never be the same again.

people's hands and asking them what their grievances were. At this stage, people were too stunned – and too scared – to speak their minds openly, but as this style became the norm, the Soviet population were to become more courageous in what they said. Conversely, Gorbachev became more reluctant to meet Soviet citizens so spontaneously, although he continued to hold walkabouts on foreign visits.

While anxious for change, Gorbachev recognized the need to proceed with caution. The old guard were still too influential for him to be able to change everything in one fell swoop. An early success came in July 1985, when he shunted

Andrei Gromyko into the largely symbolic post of Chairman of the Supreme Soviet, and put in his place as foreign minister Eduard Shevardnadze. The appointment raised many eyebrows both at home and abroad. Shevardnadze was Party leader in his native Georgia, and had been in charge of internal security in the republic, but he had no experience of foreign affairs, and spoke Russian with a heavy Georgian accent. Yet this was to prove one of the most far-reaching of Gorbachev's decisions, leading to a revolution in Soviet foreign policy.

Another highly significant change of personnel came in December of that year. Viktor

Так некоторые «перестраиваются»

Grishin was retired after 18 years as head of the Party in Moscow. His replacement was a virtual unknown, the Party boss in the Siberian city of Sverdlovsk: Boris Yeltsin. Little could Gorbachev have realized that, just as Shevardnadze's appointment was to bring about a foreign policy revolution, Yeltsin's arrival in Moscow would eventually lead to the greatest revolution in domestic affairs since 1917.

During the first year of Gorbachev's time in power, three words were constantly heard: *uskorenie, perestroika, glasnost*. The first, meaning 'acceleration,' dropped out of use as it became ever more obvious that what the Soviet Union needed was not just a speeding up of social development but a radical overhaul, or 'restructuring': *perestroika. Glasnost*, or 'openness', was considered by Gorbachev to be essential for *perestroika*. You could not begin to reform society if you did not first admit openly what society's problems were. It is impossible to overestimate the size of the task faced by Gor-

bachev in trying to implement these policies. Almost 70 years of Soviet power had seen a system and a mentality become entrenched which was corrupt, totally opposed to change and inherently secretive.

All three of these factors were evident in Gorbachev's first big test, when he had been General Secretary for just over a year. At 1.23am on 26 April 1986, a nuclear reactor at the Chernobyl Atomic Power Station in Ukraine exploded, sending a flow of radioactivity into the atmosphere which it would take almost two weeks to stem. It was to come to light that the reactor contained a basic design fault, which allowed all safety systems to be shut off. Furthermore, it was revealed that the shoddy workmanship and theft of materials which were regarded as 'normal' practices on Soviet building sites had been evident during the construction of the power station. These examples of *glasnost* took a long time to emerge. Chernobyl was not just an ecological, human and technical disaster; it was a disaster as far as openness was concerned, too.

The Chernobyl disaster was first revealed by Swedish scientists, who discovered increased levels of radiation over their country more than 48 hours after the explosion. After pressure from the Swedish government, the Soviet authorities admitted that the USSR was the source of the radiation. Instead of appealing to the outside world for help in dealing with the world's worst nuclear catastrophe, they pretended that the situation was under control. Worse still, in order to avoid panic they hid the seriousness of the accident from their own people who were directly affected by it. It was 36 hours before there was a mass evacuation of the immediate area. Thousands of others in the path of the deadly radioactive cloud, especially in the neighboring republic of Belorussia, were kept in complete ignorance of the danger they were facing.

As *glasnost* developed over the next few years, so did the tales of those who had been affected by radiation. It was not just the firefighters and soldiers who rushed to Chernobyl to put out the fire and stem the leak of radiation, thousands of others also suffered. Children were born with radiation-related deformities and, in 1990, an album of photographs was published showing what had happened to animals and plants in the area around Chernobyl. Two-headed calves and leaves one-meter across were examples of the awesome power of radiation run amok.

It took Gorbachev three weeks to respond in person to Chernobyl. His performance showed that *glasnost* was still in its infancy. He claimed that, once the authorities had received reliable and accurate information, they had passed it on to their own people and the rest of the world. This, as could be seen in later years when more was revealed about Chernobyl, was nonsense.

BELOW: On 26 April 1986 the world's worst nuclear accident happened at the Chernobyl plant in Ukraine. Once the leak of radiation from the damaged reactor number four was stemmed, the whole block was encased in a huge concrete tomb, called 'the Sarcophagus.' Here, construction of the Sarcophagus is well under way.

The authorities continued to hide anything they could.

From the early days, Gorbachev's greatest success was to be in international relations. This began in November 1985 with his first meeting with US President Ronald Reagan, in Geneva. The surprisingly cordial atmosphere created, and the one-to-one chats earned this meeting the nickname of 'the fireside summit.' Things were not always so cosy. When the two men met in Reykjavik in October of the following year, they showed greatly differing positions on arms control, so much so that there was a rift in Soviet-American relations for some months. But as this was overcome, the two sides were to develop an unprecedented level of trust and understanding. There is no doubt that, on the Soviet side, this was principally due to Gorbachev and his foreign minister, Eduard Shevardnadze.

Gorbachev's handling of the human rights issue in the first years and months was also cautious, yet positive. Hundreds of political prisoners were amnestied, although this could not be done without saying that a benevolent Soviet leadership had 'pardoned them' for their crimes – in most cases, their only crimes were thinking differently and being prepared to speak out about it. Most significantly, Gorbachev personally telephoned Andrei Sakharov and invited him back to Moscow from his internal exile in Gorky. This was a calculated risk as he knew that Sakharov would not remain silent, but he hoped that he would see the positive changes that were being made and would endorse them. While Sakharov was to exchange angry words with Gorbachev literally until the day he died, this was a gamble which paid off for Gorbachev

both politically and in terms of raising his prestige abroad.

As well as taking calculated risks, Gorbachev also showed that he was adept at taking advantage of unexpected turns of events. One such happened on 28 May 1987, when a young German named Matthias Rust managed to avoid all Soviet air defenses to fly his Cessna light aircraft right to the center of Moscow, where he landed alongside Red Square. Gorbachev used the ensuing embarrassment to sack his defense minister, Marshal Sergei Sokolov, replacing him with his preferred choice, General Dmitry Yazov. Four years later, when the attempted coup took place, Gorbachev may have wished he had chosen otherwise, since Yazov was one of the ringleaders. But in 1987 he was trumpeting the Gorbachev line loudly and clearly as commander of the Far Eastern Military District.

If the appointment of General Yazov (who was promoted to marshal in 1990) was a sign of Gorbachev's desire to make *perestroika* irreversible, an incident later in the year showed that Gorbachev still recognized the need to proceed with caution. Boris Yeltsin, who, in nearly two years as Moscow Party boss had shaken up the capital, was growing impatient with the slow pace of change. Finally, his patience snapped at the plenary meeting of the Central Committee in October, and he offered to resign.

According to the unwritten rules, senior Soviet politicians did not jump from their positions; they were either pushed or died. Yeltsin's case was put on hold while the leadership collectively buried their heads in the sand to celebrate the 70th anniversary of the revolution. Then on 9 November, Yeltsin was called from hospital to

RIGHT: US President Ronald Reagan shakes hands with General Secretary Mikhail Gorbachev at the Reykjavik Summit in October 1986. Although Reykjavik was to prove the least successful of the superpower summits of the Gorbachev era, the personal relationship which Gorbachev and Reagan developed was an important factor in the ending of the Cold War.

BELOW: Chernobyl would come back to haunt Gorbachev, and even became a symbol for Ukrainian nationalists who protested that it was brought about through Moscow's careless policies. Here, demonstrators from the Ukrainian ecological movement protest in Kiev on 26 April 1991, the fifth anniversary of the disaster.

LEFT: Recently-promoted Marshal Dmitry Yazov reviews the troops on Red Square on 9 May 1990, before the parade to mark the 45th anniversary of the victory over Nazi Germany. In 1987, Yazov was Gorbachev's choice as Defense Minister. Four years later, he was to be one of the key conspirators in the coup attempt against Gorbachev.

face a special meeting of the Moscow City Party Committee. There the 'correct' scenario was played out: one after another, party members criticized Yeltsin for his policies, his manner, his arrogance, until the man himself was forced to 'confess' to his unseemly behavior. Then, and only then, could he be sacked.

Gorbachev believed Yeltsin could still be of some use in the government, and he was moved to be first deputy chairman of the state construction committee. But the General Secretary failed to appreciate that Yeltsin had become extraordinarily popular with Muscovites. Even after his demise, Yeltsin was able to speak out in a way that no disgraced Soviet political leader ever had before, thanks to Gorbachev's own policy of *glasnost*. Even so, in November 1987 no-one would have believed that in just four years the respective roles of Yeltsin and Gorbachev could be so dramatically reversed.

1988 was to be a year of ebb and flow for *perestroika*. In March matters took a step backward, following the publication of a letter in the hardline newspaper *Sovetskaya Rossiya*. Entitled 'I

LEFT: A man who could not keep pace with *perestroika*: Yegor Ligachev was one of Gorbachev's chief sponsors for General Secretary in 1985. Yet he soon became the symbol of reaction in the Politburo. Having been given the traditional poisoned chalice of agriculture secretary, Ligachev had been retired back to his native Siberia well before the coup happened.

In June 1988, *perestroika* received a much-needed boost, when the 19th Communist Party Conference agreed that multi-candidate elections to choose a new parliament, the Congress of People's Deputies, would take place the following March. Nevertheless, the fact that this was a party decision, only later ratified by parliament, showed that it was the Communist Party which still held all the political cards. A further demonstration of this, that summer was the repression of the Democratic Union, an overtly political body which called for the establishment of a multi-party system in the USSR. Its formation in May was swiftly followed by the creation of a special riot police department, known by its Russian acronym as OMON. One of OMON's first functions was to break up Democratic Union meetings. It was to continue to play a sinister role in developments over the next three years.

A swing back in Gorbachev's favor came at a special session of parliament at the end of September. With stunning simplicity, Gorbachev oversaw the retirement of Andrei Gromyko, taking for himself the post of Chairman of the Supreme Soviet, and Yegor Ligachev was removed from his post in charge of ideology, and given the traditionally thankless task of being responsible for agriculture. As 1988 drew to a close, ominous signs were appearing for the future of the empire itself. Around the periphery, cracks were begining to show. The first of these happened in February 1988, when Armenians began to demonstrate for the return to their jurisdiction of Nagorny Karabakh from Azerbaijan. Karabakh is an enclave geographically located in Azerbaijan, but with an overwhelmingly Armenian population. On 20 February, the Karabakh parliament voted for the return of the enclave to Armenia. Eight days later, the first serious violence erupted over the Karabakh question, when Azeris went on the rampage in the town of Sumgait, in what was described as an anti-Armenian 'pogrom.' At least 32 people died.

Sporadic outbursts of violence followed all year, until martial law was declared in December. Just before this, Armenia was struck by a severe earthquake which, in a similar way to Chernobyl, showed up the deficiencies of Soviet workmanship. Nearly all of the 15,000 inhabitants of the town of Spitak perished, many of them because buildings – constructed in a known earthquake zone, and supposedly to standards to reflect this – collapsed like so many packs of cards. In all, nearly 30,000 people died, making it the most devastating earthquake in Soviet history. Unlike Chernobyl, this time the authorities immediately appealed for – and received – international help.

The Armenian earthquake also took the gloss off what was supposed to be a triumphant day at the United Nations in New York for Mikhail Gorbachev. News of the disaster came through just

ABOVE: A tiny fragment of the terrible devastation wrought by the Armenian earthquake of 7 December 1988. Some 30,000 died and thousands of others were left homeless in the worst earthquake in Soviet history.

cannot waive my principles,' it was written by a chemistry teacher in Leningrad, Nina Andreyeva. Its tone was so contrary to *perestroika*, calling for a return to 'the good old days' of Stalinism, that it was suspected that the letter at least had the support of someone at the top, particularly as Gorbachev was on an official trip abroad when it was published. In fact, Yegor Ligachev, the hardliner in charge of ideology, called in all the newspaper editors the day after publication and strongly defended the letter, going so far as to suggest that other newspapers should reflect similar views.

It was only three weeks later that *Pravda* published a rebuff to Mrs Andreyeva, and the supporters of *perestroika* breathed a huge sigh of relief. However, the underlying message was clear: the reforms were not yet irreversible. The hardline forces which had been so taken aback by the demise of the old-style leadership and the arrival of Gorbachev were clearly re-organizing.

LEFT: Mikhail Gorbachev and his wife Raisa try to comfort some of the survivors of the Armenian earthquake. Gorbachev was stunned by the way in which the survivors wanted to talk more about the situation in Nagorny Karabakh than about the disaster which had befallen them.

BELOW: Gorbachev addressing the United Nations General Assembly, 7 December 1988. Despite his announcement of a reduction in the Soviet armed forces of half a million men – which reportedly took even the Soviet military by surprise – his speech was overshadowed by the earthquake.

after he had delivered a speech in which he outlined wide-ranging unilateral cuts in the Soviet armed forces. The Soviet leader was forced to cancel the next stage of his foreign trip – a visit to London – in order to return home. From Moscow, he flew straight down to the Armenian capital, Yerevan. When he visited the earthquake zone, Gorbachev was shaken less by what he saw than by what he heard from desperate Armenians who had just lost their loved ones and their homes: they berated him about Karabakh. He returned to Moscow in high dudgeon, and it was left to Prime Minister Nikolai Ryzhkov to share the people's grief over the earthquake.

In the Baltic states of Estonia, Latvia and Lithuania, 1988 saw the growth of serious nationalist movements. Even at the height of Brezhnev's rule, when Andropov had taught Soviet citizens that respect and fear for the KGB were essential if you wanted a quiet life, it was an open secret

that the majority of the Balts resented being a part of the Soviet Union. The secret protocols to the Nazi-Soviet Pact of 1939 (which granted the USSR control over the Baltic States) could never be discussed publicly; but every Balt was brought up to know of their existence.

In the first three years of Gorbachev and *perestroika*, the Balts were as skeptical as anyone that the new Soviet leader wanted to build society on different foundations. By 1988 the frontiers of *glasnost* were being pushed further back, and on 13 April Estonian television screened a live debate in which the question of a valid opposition to the Communist Party was openly discussed.

The seed flourished rapidly into an organized movement, the Popular Front for *Perestroika*. Within two months the movement had 50,000 members in a republic with a population of just 1.5 million. The other two Baltic states, Latvia

LEFT: Armenia's grief. A woman in Leninakan, near the heart of the earthquake, weeps for her lost loved ones.

BELOW: US Presidents present and future, Reagan and Bush, with Gorbachev in New York, December 1988. George Bush seemed easily to pick up the Reagan baton in the superpower relationship; but after the collapse of the Soviet Union some criticized the way in which he moved just as smoothly to a relationship with Russian President Boris Yeltsin.

and Lithuania, quickly followed Estonia's lead: popular fronts were formed and grew rapidly.

In November the Estonian parliament declared the republic's sovereignty. For the time being, though, this was still within the Soviet Union. At the end of 1988, everyone knew that full independence was on the minds of the Balts but, with the thought that overly hasty actions could precipitate the use of force by the Kremlin, the Baltic leaders held back from stating the obvious conclusion of their actions. The events of 1989 were to change all that.

10
1989-THE YEAR OF TURMOIL

LEFT: 1989 was the year that Communism was toppled in the Second Empire. Following the Rumanian Revolution of December of that year, Lenin's statue was removed from his pedestal in the center of Bucharest in March 1990.

When the end of the greater Soviet empire came, with the collapse of Communism in the second empire, it was stunningly swift and relatively painless. The pain was to come later, as the newly independent countries of Central and Eastern Europe tried to re-establish democratic traditions that had been suppressed for over 40 years, or to create democracies where none had previously existed. The speed with which Eastern Europe threw off Communism, compared with the more difficult process in the Soviet Union itself, reflected the way in which the system had been established in those two parts of the empire. Communism had been imposed on the second empire from without at the end of World War II because of geography. There was no ideological reason why these countries should have become Communist. Russia, on the other hand, had brought Communism upon itself. It had had its own revolution, led by one of its own sons, Lenin.

BELOW: Despite the dramatic changes in Eastern Europe, in Moscow traditional events continued, giving a veneer of continuity in a troubled land.

It was an extraordinary feature of Soviet life in the latter part of Brezhnev's rule that foreigners who tried to join in conversations (in private) in which the system was being criticized often found themselves being rounded on, even though they were agreeing with the sentiments being expressed. 'What right do you have to criticize? This system is *ours*!', was heard all too often. Whether they liked the system or not, Soviet people gained a perverse pride from the idea that they had given the world something which, for all its shortcomings, had been adopted, willingly or otherwise, by millions of people worldwide.

The beginning of the end for Communism in Hungary came in May 1988, when Janos Kadar, who had been installed as leader following the 1956 uprising, was ousted by his own Hungarian Socialist Workers' Party. Throughout the Seventies and Eighties Hungary had been quietly building its own version of socialism. This was done without much fuss, so as to avoid rocking the boat and possibly causing another Soviet intervention, but by the time that Mikhail Gorbachev started to encourage *glasnost* in the Soviet Union in 1985, Hungary had already set off down that path. Hungary saw more clearly than any other Eastern European country how to use this new policy in Moscow to its own advantage.

Behind the new leader, Karoly Grosz, there were others in the leadership with a far-reaching perception of what needed to be done to bring real progress to Hungary. Chief among these was Imre Pozsgay. It was he who really started the ball rolling that was to destroy the system in January 1989. Firstly, he took advantage of Grosz's absence on a foreign visit to describe multi-party elections as 'a noble contest.' This was more than a year before the Communist Party of the Soviet Union was to agree to renounce its monopoly of power, and so was heresy to the orthodox Communist.

As if to emphasize that he was proposing the collapse of the old order, later that month Pozsgay destroyed another sacred cow when he declared that the events of 1956 had not been a 'counter-revolution' as the official version had it, but a popular uprising. For any observer outside the Communist bloc, that was stating the obvious; but inside it, it was a blow to the very legitimacy of the regime. Communism was supposed to represent the will of the people. Admitting that some 30 years earlier it had done exactly the opposite was tantamount to saying that the regime that had been established by Soviet tanks was one enormous mistake.

From this point, Communism's demise in Hungary now seems inevitable. In June 1989 the remains of Imre Nagy, the people's hero of 1956, were exhumed from their unmarked grave and buried with full state ceremony. Later in the summer Hungary was to allow thousands of East

Germans to flee from Communism across its borders, and when free elections were finally held in March 1990, Communism was extinguished for all but a few dreamers who still believed that the mistakes of the past could be corrected.

Pozsgay and his colleagues were to learn the meaning of the saying that the prophet is never honored in his own country. They had hoped that people would flock to their re-vamped socialist party out of gratitude for their revelations about the sins of the past. But, 34 years after they had first tried, in 1990 the Hungarian people wanted to get rid of socialism and Communism for good.

In Poland, as in Hungary, Communism ended with a whimper rather than a bang. The build-up had a strong sense of *déja-vu*: the economy in chaos, strikes, and the authorities forced into negotiating with the Solidarity trade union. After the complete lifting of martial law in 1983, General Wojciech Jarulzelski was forced to deal with the problem faced by any would-be military ruler: seizing power with the help of the army is comparatively easy, because it is a military matter; but maintaining it is a political problem, not a strength of most generals.

By the late 1980s the Polish economy was in as great a mess as it had been 10 years earlier. Soon after the outbreak of pro-Solidarity strikes in August 1988, the government had to concede that it would have to open negotiations with the opposition. In January 1989, Solidarity was legalized once more (it had been banned when martial law was imposed in December 1981). Within a few months, the Polish United Workers' Party agreed to power-sharing with Solidarity, and elections were set for parliament, the Sejm, and the newly-constituted senate in June.

© Richard Natkiel, 1993

ABOVE: The Soviet sphere of influence in Eastern Europe, 1945-89.

LEFT: After the trials and tribulations of the previous nine years, Poland's was one of the smoothest transitions away from socialism in 1989. Lech Walesa, leader of Solidarity and destined to be Poland's first post-Communist President, acknowledges admirers in Washington in November 1989.

As it turned out, the elections were probably just too early for Solidarity to assert itself fully. The 'trade union' – by now, nothing less than a fully-fledged political party – agreed to allow two-thirds of the seats in the Sejm to remain in Communist hands, but in those seats where there was a free vote, the rejection of Communism by the people was almost total. All the remaining one-third of seats in the Sejm went to Solidarity candidates, as did all but one seat in the senate. Two months later, in August, General Jarulzelski was forced to put another nail into Communism's Polish coffin, when he appointed Solidarity's Tadeusz Mazowiecki as prime minister, the first non-Communist head of government in Eastern Europe since the 1940s.

After the crushing of the Prague Spring in 1968, Moscow considered that its two most reliable allies in the second empire were East Germany and Czechoslovakia. The Kremlin was confident that in the event of any military conflict in Central Europe between NATO and the Warsaw Pact, East Germany and Czechoslovakia would need the least encouragement to fight, as it would be their own territory they would be defending. Politically, too, the Soviet Union believed it could rely on these two countries. After all, it was the leaderships of East Germany and Czechoslovakia which had protested the loudest about the rise of Solidarity.

The decision by the governments of both East Germany and Czechoslovakia to ignore the significance of the changes going on around them was a major contributory factor to the swift destruction of Communism in both countries in 1989. Even if the two governments had tried to accommodate these changes, they could not have prevented their systems being swept aside by the inevitable tide of 40 years of frustration, coupled with the removal of the fear that had kept the system in place.

By mid-1989, the East German and Czechoslovak leaderships were worried about developments in Hungary and Poland, and, as in 1956, 1968 and 1980, feared the spread of democratic ideas across their borders. More worrying for them still, though, was that this time the Soviet Union seemed ready to sit back and do nothing to stop it. This seemed to be confirmed when Soviet leader Mikhail Gorbachev appeared to renounce the so-called 'Brezhnev doctrine,' which claimed to give the USSR the right to intervene to protect socialism in its satellites. Speaking before the Parliamentary Assembly of the Council of Europe in Strasbourg in July 1989, Gorbachev declared that there must be 'no use or threat of force . . . within alliances.'

That same month, East German fears began to be realized. East German citizens who were holidaying in supposedly fraternal Hungary found

that they were not being prevented from crossing the border with Austria. From there, it was just a short drive to West Germany. As news of this spread, the trickle quickly became a flood. For form's sake, the Hungarians turned back a few, but, in September, they allowed the Germans to go officially.

This exodus began on the eve of a supposedly grand occasion, since on 7 October the German Democratic Republic was to mark its 40th birthday. On the 6th, Gorbachev flew to Berlin, and appeared to give some hope to the desperate regime by emphasizing the importance of maintaining 'postwar realities' – in other words, the division of Germany – for keeping the peace in Europe. But the following day, the GDR's official birthday celebrations were marred by unofficial demonstrations in Berlin and Leipzig, calling for the overthrow of the system and even unification with West Germany.

After Gorbachev's departure, the demonstrations continued. It was in Leipzig that the showdown was to take place. On 9 October all foreign journalists were banned from the city. It later emerged that people's worst fears were justified: a decision had been taken to use force to suppress that night's, and all subsequent demonstrations, once and for all.

Only five months earlier, the peoples of Eastern Europe had had a sobering reminder that this could still be the way in which Communist regimes would deal with dissent. On 3 June 1989, the tanks of the Chinese People's Liberation Army rolled against pro-democracy demonstrators in Peking's Tiananmen Square. Thousands died, and, despite the publicity given by worldwide television coverage of the events, no-one was able to lift a finger to help the demonstrators. In Leipzig, the East German authorities were planning their own 'Tiananmen,' but without the publicity.

ABOVE: Solidarity supporters, Warsaw, December 1990. Once freedom has been gained, Solidarity found it harder to maintain unity as a ruling force.

BELOW: Kiss of death? East German leader Erich Honecker greets Gorbachev.

In the end, the order to use force was rescinded at the last minute. This was possibly because the authorities recognized that their gamble had failed. As word spread that this was the plan, more and more people gathered in the Nikolaikirche for the by now traditional church service before the demonstration. This showed clearly that the regime's main prop – fear – was disintegrating fast. Not only did the demonstration go ahead, but the armed militias who had been sent on to the streets to disperse the crowds ended up in animated conversations with them.

After 9 October, there could be no turning back. Even the replacement of Erich Honecker as leader of the Socialist Unity Party by Egon Krenz was no more than superficial. The West German embassy in Prague was now besieged by East Germans seeking a passage to the West. The GDR closed its border with Czechoslovakia, but on 3 November, having already re-opened the border, East Germans were allowed to leave via Czechoslovakia.

If citizens were being allowed to leave the country by an indirect route, the only logical conclusion could be that a direct route would soon be opened. On 9 November it was, as joyous crowds on both sides of the Berlin Wall began physically tearing down the most vivid symbol of the division of Europe. From that moment, not only was the Communist regime effectively dead in East Germany, but unification with the West became inevitable, even though the formalities were to take another 11 months to complete.

The people of Czechoslovakia were greatly encouraged by events in East Germany. The latent opposition movement had already begun to show itself as early as August 1988, when

demonstrations were organized to mark the 20th anniversary of the crushing of the Prague Spring, but it had by no means been plain sailing from then on. Following a large demonstration in Prague in January 1989, the leaders were arrested and imprisoned. Among them was the writer Vaclav Havel. As he sat in jail during the first half of 1989, neither he nor anyone else could have imagined that he would end the year as Czechoslovakia's acting president.

Gorbachev's renunciation of the Brezhnev doctrine in July was followed in October by another highly significant comment by Gorbachev's Press spokesman, Gennady Gerasimov. Gerasimov's apparently witty aside that the Soviet Union had replaced the Brezhnev doctrine by the 'Sinatra doctrine' – everyone can choose to do it 'My Way' – was understood in Czechoslovakia as an acknowledgement that, whatever happened there, there would be no repeat of 1968.

If Leipzig on 9 October was to be the crucial day in the GDR, Prague on 17 November was to be the watershed for Czechoslovakia. Although the authorities did not use firearms against a mass demonstration, baton-wielding militiamen

did try to persuade democrats to drop their protests. As in East Germany, the tactic had the opposite effect. However much the militia tried to cow the opposition into submission, the numbers demonstrating grew, because the people of Czechoslovakia had stopped being afraid. No Communist regime can last long if its citizens are not afraid of it.

Ten days after the Prague demonstration, three-quarters of the workforce of Czechoslovakia took part in a general strike. The pressure on the government was too great. In the smoothest transition in the second empire, power passed from the Communists to the democrats. Czechoslovakia was lucky in two respects. Firstly, of all the countries of Central and Eastern Europe, it was the one which had the strongest traditions of democracy. Even though these had been stamped on first by Nazi Germany in 1938, and then by Soviet Communism after World War II, they had not been totally eradicated.

Secondly, in Vaclav Havel Czechoslovakia was blessed with the most appealing and able post-Communist leader in the region. Although he and his colleagues were to prove naive in some areas – such as promising that they would stop the sale of Czech-produced arms on world markets, until they realized just how valuable these arms were as an export – Havel came across to his own people and to the rest of the world as a man who, having been thrust into the political limelight, would do all he could for the betterment of Czechoslovakia, not Vaclav Havel.

As revolutionary fervor gripped the northern and central countries of the second empire in 1989, the two countries in the southeastern corner, Rumania and Bulgaria, were largely ignored. There were historical reasons for this. Since the empire had been established after World War II, East Germany, Poland, Czechoslovakia and Hungary had all experienced serious social unrest, necessitating the intervention of Soviet tanks (or, in Poland's case, self-imposed martial law). Such opposition to Soviet domination had passed by Rumania and Bulgaria.

Rumania had asserted its independence from the Soviet Union by refusing to have Soviet troops stationed on its soil, but as the country did not border on a NATO country, nor act as a crucial supply route for Soviet troops, this did not affect Soviet strategic planning too drastically. Furthermore, in constructing this supposedly independent state, Rumanian leader Nicolae Ceausescu had created a monstrous regime which repressed its own people far more even than the Soviet Union. There was no danger that Rumania would 'infect' its neighbors with ideas of freedom or democracy.

Bulgaria's ties to the USSR – and, more especially, to Russia – were strong. There had long been a genuine affinity between these two Slav nations. In 1878 the Russians had helped liberate Bulgaria from Turkish rule under the Ottoman empire. And Bulgaria was the one country in Eastern Europe where the feeling was widespread that in 1944 the Russians had liberated

RIGHT: The Wall is breached! West Berliners celebrate the first free crossing of East Berliners for over 28 years; 10 November 1989.

LEFT: Czechoslovak reformers past and present: Vaclav Havel (right), the writer who was imprisoned as a dissident in 1989 yet ended the year as President of Czechoslovakia, embraces Alexander Dubcek, leader of the Prague Spring, crushed by Soviet tanks in 1968. The announcement had just been made of the resignation of the Czechoslovak government, 24 November 1989.

them again, rather than conquered them. In the mid-1960s and again in the late 1970s, the Bulgarian leader Todor Zhivkov had even applied to the Soviet Union to incorporate Bulgaria as the sixteenth republic of the Union. Leonid Brezhnev was able to see that any personal aggrandize-ment this might bring would not be worth the international reprobation, as the outside world would find it impossible to believe that country should willingly apply to join the Soviet Union.

So despite the upheavals in the rest of the second empire, little was expected from Bulgaria

RIGHT: Wenceslas Square, Prague. Czechoslovaks celebrate the overthrow of Communism in November 1989. The sign hung round the neck of the battered statue of Stalin reads 'Nothing lasts forever.'

BELOW: In the days before the Czechoslovak government resigned, pressure was mounting thanks to peaceful protests in Prague. Candles were lit as a symbol of hope.

or Rumania, but even in these states the tide of change proved unstoppable. In Bulgaria, it was surprisingly simple. Todor Zhivkov tried to divert criticism away from his growing incompetence by making Bulgaria's large Turkish minority a scapegoat for the country's ills. He took away their rights as an ethnic minority. By doing so, he provoked the anger of Turkey, the Soviet Union

LEFT: Continuing signs of unrest in Bulgaria. Here, the police protest.

and his own Politburo, who had been ignored in the decision-making process. Following Zhivkov's political misjudgment regarding the Turkish minority events moved quickly, leading to his eventual replacement.

In November 1989, Bulgarian Foreign Minister Petar Mladenov stopped off in Moscow on his way back from an official visit to China. Here, he

BELOW: From dissident to President. The election of Vaclav Havel as Czechoslovak President in December 1989 was greeted with genuine popular joy.

RIGHT: Trial of a dictator: Rumanian television pictures of the impromptu trial of Nicolae Ceausescu and his wife Elena, on 25 December 1989. Ceausescu refused to take any part in the proceedings, and is shown here stopping his wife from answering a question. Immediately after the trial, the pair were taken out and shot (below).

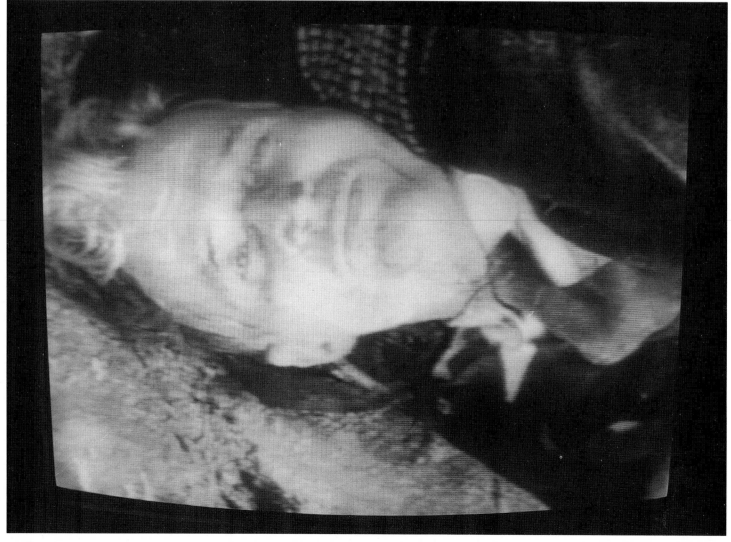

received official confirmation that it was time for Zhivkov to go. At a session of the Bulgarian Communist Party's Central Committee later that month, a stunned Zhivkov was replaced as General Secretary by Mladenov. He restored the ethnic rights of the Turks, and announced that the country would move toward multi-party elections. These took place in June 1990. Although the Communists, under the guise of the Bulgarian Socialist Party, won control, they were now left largely to stand on their own two feet. Soviet patronage – or domination, depending on your point of view – was over.

Events were nothing like as simple or as peaceful in Rumania. As 1989 drew to a close, it seemed that the tremendous events which had occurred in all the other five countries really had passed by Rumania. Then, on 17 December, in the town of Timisoara, near the Hungarian border, crowds gathered to try and defend the Hungarian pastor Laszlo Tokes, who had locked himself in his church in a defiant gesture to prevent the authorities evicting him. Tanks were sent in and a massacre took place.

Suddenly the Rumanian people were not lying down. Trouble spread throughout the region, and troops began to go over to the opposition side. On 21 December, Ceausescu addressed what should have been an obedient crowd from the balcony of party headquarters in Bucharest. The chant rose, hesitantly at first, of Timisoara. Ceausescu and his power-crazed wife, Elena, fled, but were captured and, after a summary trial, executed on Christmas Day. Rumania was gripped by a bloody, but short revolution. When it was over, many of the former Communists had changed colors sufficiently to take over power as the National Salvation Front, though its future was much in doubt.

Even though large question marks remained over the chances for the development of democracy in Rumania, the overthrow of Ceausescu meant that by the end of 1989 the second empire established by Stalin in the late 1940s had collapsed. Far from attempting to intervene to prevent it, the Soviet Union almost seemed glad to be rid of the encumberance that the empire proved to be. Certainly it meant that the Soviet leadership was able to devote more time and energy to dealing with its own internal problems. As 1989 showed, these problems were such that even in the Soviet Union the death knell was already beginning to toll for Communism itself.

BELOW: Although the Zhivkov government's poor treatment of the Bulgarian Turks was ultimately one of the reasons for its downfall, the lot of the Bulgarian Turks did not improve dramatically afterward. This rally calling for full rights for the Turks took place in the town of Krdzhali in March 1991.

11

TROUBLES AT HOME

LEFT: 'Yeltsin represents socialism Lenin-style!
Vote for Yeltsin!' runs a banner at a big pro-
Yeltsin rally in Moscow on the eve of elections
to the new Congress of People's Deputies.

The reaction of the Soviet people to what was going on in Eastern Europe in 1989 was mixed: diehard Communists were appalled; liberals and nationalists seeking independence for their republics were excited. Most people were somewhat bewildered by it, and too concerned with their own problems to give it much thought. At the same time as the East Europeans were ditching Communism, the Soviet Union was certainly beset with plenty of problems of its own.

The years 1989 and 1990 were characterized in the Soviet Union by swings of the pendulum from democratic reform back to repressive Communism, but with each swing toward liberalization, more and more credence was taken away from the Communist Party. By the end of 1990 it was clear that the only way in which it could prop up its crumbling regime was by force.

An important – if far from total – breakthrough for democracy came in March 1989 with the elections to the USSR's new parliament, the Congress of People's Deputies. For the first time, there were multi-candidate elections for many seats, but there was still no choice of parties. It was to be almost another year before the Communist Party was to agree to the removal of Article Six from the Soviet Constitution, the clause which gave the party the leading role in society and effectively banned all other political parties. In practice, of course, a number of candidates represented other political views, but all those standing continued to be labeled as 'party' (ie Communist) and 'non-party.'

The party made sure that it had a safe majority in the Congress by insisting that one-third of all seats went to 'safe' organizations, such as the Central Committee, the youth organization, Komosomol, and the Writers' Union. Here there was no contest, and it was in the Central Committee that Mikhail Gorbachev opted for a safe passage to the Congress, by standing as one of 100 candidates for a guaranteed 100 seats.

With his popularity declining, as *perestroika* continued to fail to produce any improvement in living standards, this would probably have been Gorbachev's last chance to submit himself to a popular vote and win. His decision not to do this was to count against him in future battles with the genuinely popular Boris Yeltsin. Yeltsin not only stood as one of three candidates in his Moscow constituency, but was returned to the Congress with a massive 89 percent of the vote.

Before the Congress assembled for the first time on 25 May, there was a sobering reminder that this exercise in democracy did not mean that the Soviet Union had now adopted democratic methods to deal with its citizens. In early April, a huge pro-independence demonstration gathered in the Georgian capital Tbilisi. The protesters conducted themselves peacefully, but showed no sign of moving from the steps of the parliament building until they received some satisfaction.

The demonstration was into its fifth day when the authorities swooped. In the early hours of 9 April, troops in armored personnel carriers bore down on the crowd. The pincers-like movement, designed to cut off escape routes, was a clear indication that this was not simply an action designed to clear the area. Moscow was punishing the Georgians for daring to call for the overthrow of Soviet rule. Troops waded into the crowds wielding sharpened shovels and spraying poison gas – 21 people, mostly women, died; hundreds more were wounded.

The Tbilisi massacre remained one of the great unpunished crimes of the Soviet era. A question about what had really happened was the first matter put to the opening session of Congress, and damning reports were produced

BELOW: Boris Yeltsin casts his vote in the March 1989 elections for the Congress of People's Deputies. The man who had returned from the political wilderness, following his expulsion from the Communist Party's Politburo in November 1987, was elected to one of the Moscow seats by a landslide.

the last time that Soviet troops were used to deal with those seeking independence from the USSR.

The pendulum swung back toward democracy when the Congress opened, if only because there was live television coverage of the proceedings. Even though Gorbachev could physically silence Andrei Sakharov by switching off the microphone when the academician started talking about the abolition of the party's leading role, the action was witnessed by millions of people.

This democracy (of sorts) so grabbed the attention of the Soviet population that a 20 percent drop in industrial output was attributed to people watching the Congress. To the Communists' great relief, because of this it was decided that in future only certain debates would be shown live, with edited highlights of the rest. Ironically, by the time this came into effect, people had stopped watching anyway, believing that the parliament had become a place where there was much talk but no action.

The real news was happening outside the Kremlin. On 10 July, miners in the huge Siberian coalfields of Kuzbass went on strike, demanding better living conditions. They were soon joined by fellow miners in Karaganda (in Kazakhstan), Vorkuta (in the north) and the Donbass (in Eastern Ukraine). It was the biggest industrial action ever taken in the Soviet Union. Gorbachev tried

LEFT: Remembering the Tbilisi massacre. A year to the day after Soviet troops killed 21 people in the Georgian capital, Tbilisi, on 9 April 1989, a mother helps her son to place a candle beside the memorial in the Georgian cultural center in Moscow. The *bas-relief* shows a soldier attacking a woman with a sharpened shovel, the way in which most of the dead perished.

BELOW: A demonstration to mark the first anniversary of the massacre on 9 April 1990 in Tbilisi. Far from crushing the independence movement in Georgia, the massacre served to galvanize those forces wanting to break away from the Soviet Union.

by both the Soviet and the Georgian parliamentary commissions set up to look into the issue. But no-one was ever made to answer for the decision to send in the troops, or the fact that they behaved in such a brutal fashion. Nor was it to be

1989 saw more demonstrations than ever before in Soviet history. As the people found their voice, displays of national feeling such as this one (right) in Kiev, Ukraine, became a familiar sight. The banner calling for the rehabilitation of the Ukrainian language is written in Ukrainian and, unusually, in Hebrew. But the state continued to put on its official parades, such as for Revolution Day on 7 November (far right).

BELOW: In September, a huge rally took place in the Western Ukrainian city of Lvov, as a protest against the occupation of Western Ukraine by Soviet troops 50 years earlier. It also gave Catholics the chance to call for the re-legalization of their church.

to argue that the strikes were in support of *perestroika*, but then blamed anti-Communists for trying to manipulate them for their own political ends. That the strike was principally an economic one seemed to be borne out by the miners' decision to return to work in exchange for promises of better conditions, but the miners had realized that they could also be a political force to be reckoned with.

Elsewhere in the country, ethnic strife was spreading. In June, there were violent clashes in the Fergana valley in Uzbekistan, as Uzbeks fought with Meskhetian Turks, descendants of people whom Stalin had deported there from Transcaucasia in World War II. Peaceful, but impassioned, demonstrations were taking place in the southwestern republic of Moldavia, calling for the return of the Latin script for their language. (Stalin had imposed the Cyrillic script in an attempt to Sovietize the Rumanian language it really was.) Not only did the Moldavian parliament pass a law to this effect, it even changed the name of the republic to the Rumanian 'Moldova.'

Nowhere was the move for independence stronger than in the Baltic states. On 27 July 1989, the Supreme Soviet – the permanently sitting 'upper chamber' of the Congress of People's Deputies – even bowed to the pressure of the fast-growing reality and granted the Balts independence in economic decision-making. A month later, on 23 August, Balts marked the 50th

RIGHT: If Moscow refused to pay attention to demonstrations in the non-Russian republics, there were those who were prepared to argue their point on the streets of the capital. Here, Armenians, unhappy over handling of the dispute with Azerbaijan over Nagorny Karabakh, protest outside the Lenin Library in Moscow, on the eve of the Revolution Day celebrations (for which the banner of Lenin was put up).

anniversary of the signing of the Nazi-Soviet Pact by forming a human chain linking the three capitals of Tallinn, Riga and Vilnius. Moscow had tried to defuse this protest by allowing the newspaper *Argumenty i Fakty* to publish the secret protocols to the pact, under the terms of which Estonia, Latvia and Lithuania had become a part of the Soviet Union. After years of Soviet denials of the existence of the protocols,

when everyone in the Baltic states knew about them, this was much too little, too late.

Even in Ukraine, Russia's Slav brother, calls for independence were growing disturbingly loud for Moscow. In September, tens of thousands turned out in the western Ukrainian city of Lvov in protest at the 50th anniversary of the occupation of the region by Soviet troops. Though worrying for the central authorities, this was not too great a shock. Even at the height of Soviet power, Ukrainian nationalism had always been strong – beneath the surface at least – in western Ukraine. Of greater concern to the Kremlin was the founding congress that same month in the Ukrainian capital, Kiev, of the pro-independence movement Rukh.

Although there were some concessions to Ukrainian sentiments in Kiev – a few shop signs, courses at the university taught in Ukrainian – the city had long had a strong Russian feel to it. As you traveled farther east, Russian influence grew ever stronger. What Rukh was managing to do by late 1989 was to revive Ukrainian nationalism in areas where it had long been dormant. Ukraine had a population of 50 million, and some of the best arable land and mineral deposits in the Soviet Union. The men in the Kremlin knew only too well that, while they could try to preserve a Soviet Union without the Baltic states, it would be impossible without Ukraine.

By the fall of 1989, Gorbachev was caught in a battle between the reformers whom he had encouraged by *perestroika*, and Communist hardliners who were products of the same system that had brought him to power. In October, he tried to rein in the liberal press – in complete contradiction of *glasnost* – when he demanded the sacking of the editor of *Argumenty i Fakty*, Vladislav Starkov. Starkov's 'crime' was to publish an opinion poll which showed that Sakharov and Yeltsin were among the most popular deputies in the Congress, whilst he, Gorbachev, did not get a mention. Starkov's colleagues stood by him. Gorbachev lost.

The Communist Party met more defiance on its holiest of days, 7 November, the anniversary of the revolution. As well as the statutory official parades, unofficial protests took place in many big cities. While the Communists were celebrating 72 supposedly glorious years of socialist power, a phrase which seemed to capture better the mood of the people was '72 years on the road to nowhere!'

The party's Central Committee reacted angrily. Their protests at what they alleged was growing anarchy were stalled at their plenary meeting in December only by Gorbachev's threat to resign. By this stage, the Central Committee knew only too well that no-one else could be chosen from their ranks as an alternative leader to Gorbachev.

But on 14 December, the reformers were dealt a severe blow. It had been a day of fierce debate in the Supreme Soviet, and Gorbachev had once again publicly crossed swords with Andrei Sakharov over the abolition of the party's leading role. Sakharov went home to prepare a further speech in support of this now vital issue. It was never delivered; while working on the speech, Andrei Sakharov died of a heart attack. The country was stunned. Sakharov had come to be

regarded as the conscience of the nation, the man who had dared to speak out against the system when all around him people saw what he saw but remained silent. Some 100,000 people turned out in Moscow for his funeral. Most of them were united by the sentiment: 'Forgive us, Andrei Dmitrevich.'

The start of 1990 was marked by fresh trouble in Transcaucasia. The problem of Nagorny Karabakh had rumbled on throughout 1989. Moscow's attempt to mediate by taking the enclave under its direct rule had been deemed a failure, and control had been returned to Azerbaijan. In January 1990, groups of Azeris went on the rampage in Baku, carrying out pogroms against scores of Armenians who had decided to remain. From Moscow's point of view, the trouble became really serious when a mass demonstration in the city on 18 January called for

ABOVE: The man who came to be known as 'the conscience of the nation,' Andrei Sakharov, casts his vote in the elections to the Congress. Sakharov was to cross swords with Gorbachev in the Congress (and in the higher body, the Supreme Soviet) right up to the day he died on 14 December 1989.

RIGHT: Boris Yeltsin pays his last respects to Sakharov during the lying in state. With Yeltsin is Galina Starovoitova, a leading reformist politician. An estimated 100,000 people turned out for Sakharov's funeral.

the resignation of the government and an end to Communist rule.

The troops which had already been drafted into the area were now put on high alert. Late on the 19th, they went into action. They gave no quarter; anyone who did not get out of the way was crushed by the tanks, while others were shot. At least 100 people died. The action did not help the Armenians, in Baku or in Karabakh, but it did save Communist power in Azerbaijan.

Communist power was under a different sort of attack in the Baltic states and in Moscow. The Lithuanian Communist Party declared itself independent from the Communist Party of the Soviet Union, prompting Gorbachev to fly to Vilnius in January. He tried to reason with both the

RIGHT: A bloody start to 1990. Following massive pro-independence demonstrations in the capital of Azerbaijan, Baku, the Soviet Army moved in. At least 100 people died, including these victims lying in Baku's main hospital. They were either shot or crushed by tanks.

republic's leaders and its citizens on the streets, but ended up arguing and returned to Moscow angry and seemingly powerless to stem the tide of independence.

In Moscow, reformers called for a demonstration to take place on 4 February. Permission was granted for the demonstrators to march on Manege Square, just off Red Square and bordering the Kremlin. Moscow – so used to stage-managed celebrations on the great Communist holidays – had never seen anything like it. Tens of thousands turned out, many of them reiterating Sakharov's call for the abolition of Article Six and the leading role of the party. Reacting to the public mood, the next day Gorbachev proposed to the party's Central Committee that Article Six be abolished, as if it were his own idea.

With the removal of the party's monopoly of power, Gorbachev's thoughts were now on establishing a new form of leadership in his crumbling empire. He wanted to introduce the post of president, modeled loosely along the lines of the American presidency. There was no question but that he would be the first incumbent of such a post. The only question to be decided, once the Supreme Soviet had agreed to the principle, was should the president be elected by parliament or by the people? In the end, Gorbachev was to choose the less risky

LEFT AND BELOW: Lithuanians in their capital, Vilnius, prepare for the visit of Gorbachev in January 1990. The Soviet leader came with the intention of telling the local leadership to toe Moscow's line. He left angry with the intransigence he had encountered.

option, and on 13 March 1990, the Supreme Soviet elected Mikhail Gorbachev first (and, as history was to prove, last) president of the USSR.

ABOVE: Yeltsin's supporters in the Russian Supreme Soviet celebrate his election as parliamentary chairman, 29 May 1990.

FAR RIGHT: Lenin would not have approved. Thousands of Azeris gather in Baku's main square beneath a statue of the leader of the Revolution in a meeting of mourning, following the Baku massacre of January 1990.

Two days before Gorbachev became Soviet president, the Lithuanian parliament decreed that the USSR now had not 15 but 14 republics: Lithuania was independent. Moscow did not take the declaration seriously. Two weeks later, Soviet troops occupied former Communist Party buildings in Vilnius. When the Lithuanians did not back down, the center imposed an economic blockade on the republic. The game of cat and mouse continued until, on 29 June, the Lithuanian parliament announced that it was ready to freeze the independence declaration for 100 days from the start of official talks with Moscow.

Away from the Baltic states, in the first few months of 1990 there was more ethnic violence in Central Asia and Nagorny Karabakh; nationalist movements grew stronger in Ukraine, Moldova and Georgia; and serious rumblings of discontent became louder in Russia itself. These reached a new peak on 29 May, when Boris Yeltsin was elected chairman of the Russian parliament. Yeltsin had been voted into the new parliament two months earlier from his old home territory of Sverdlovsk in the Urals. His majority

was almost as large as that for the all-Union Congress of People's Deputies a year earlier.

On 12 June, the Russian parliament took a crucial decision, when it decreed that Russian laws took priority over Soviet laws on Russian territory. This started a flood of declarations of 'sovereignty' from the republics. After all, if Russia, the largest and most powerful republic was prepared to ignore the jurisdiction of the Soviet Union, why should any other republic behave differently? With the exception of the Baltic states (each of which considered itself 'independent' by this stage), every republic was to declare its sovereignty.

The fact that no-one really knew what this meant illustrated the absurd situation that the country was falling into. If republics really could make all their own decisions and ignore Soviet ones, then the Soviet Union had already *de facto* ceased to exist, but the Soviet power structure remained in place, and, crucially, so did the security apparatus of the Army, the interior ministry and the KGB. The Soviet leadership knew that it could still assert its authority on any part of the USSR if it so desired.

By now even Gorbachev was no longer in control of events. The changes which he had set in motion had gathered such momentum that he was no longer dictating them but simply reacting to them. Nevertheless, he still tried to give the impression that he was the master of the situation. At the Twenty-eighth Congress of the party in July he announced that a new union treaty was needed to redefine the relationship between the center and the republics. Had he made the suggestion even six months earlier, he might have won widespread support in the republics, but by the summer of 1990 the mood had moved on from this. With his popularity falling, Gorbachev was fast becoming the prophet who was not welcome in his own country.

The Twenty-eighth Congress was a watershed for the Communist Party. Attempts at showing that the party was still united were blown apart by the dramatic public resignation of Boris Yeltsin from the party. Trying to give the impression that the reluctance of many party members to accept reform had driven him to a spontaneous act, Yeltsin took the podium and declared his contempt for the Communist Party and his resignation from it. With that, he stormed out of the hall. The waiting car suggested that the action had, in fact, been well planned in advance; but it was still great theater and left delegates reeling.

After the Congress, people left the party in droves. According to official figures, 15 times more people left in 1990 than had in 1989, but these figures did not reveal the full story. In direct contravention of party rules, local organizations refused to cross off their list of members those who simply stopped paying their

ABOVE: By the summer of
1990, ethnic violence
had spread to Central
Asia.

BELOW: Soviet Foreign
Minister Eduard
Shevardnadze. In the
West he was hailed as
one of those who helped
end the Cold War.

dues. On paper, the party still had about 16 million members by the end of 1990 (down from a peak in the late Eighties of 19 million). Though impossible to assess completely accurately, in reality membership was probably in the region of 10 to 12 million.

Just as a confrontation between the Soviet Union and Russia, Gorbachev versus Yeltsin, seemed to be increasingly likely, an extraordinary thing happened: in August the two men announced that they were to cooperate on a radical economic reform program. For a month, this bizarre marriage of convenience looked as if it might work: the Soviet and Russian economies were to be reformed in just 500 days, following the radical prescription of economists Stanislav Shatalin and Grigory Yavlinsky

In September, reality intruded on this dream. The Soviet government, led by Prime Minister Nikolai Ryzhkov, announced an alternative, more cautious reform plan. Still believing that he could balance the two sides, Gorbachev proposed that the plans be amalgamated. Yeltsin described such an idea as 'like trying to mate a hedgehog with a snake.' The last chance for cooperation between the two most powerful men in the Soviet Union – if, indeed, it had really been a chance at all – had gone. Ever defiant, Yeltsin tried to introduce the 500-day plan in Russia but by day 10 it had died, quietly and un-mourned.

As far as Yeltsin was concerned, Gorbachev's attempt to reconcile the two sides meant that he was no longer in the reformers' camp. The hard-liners seized on this, too and, as the year drew to its close, they began to gain the upper hand. A clear indication of this was the replacement of Vadim Bakatin, the reform-minded Interior Minister, by the uncompromising Boris Pugo. Another was a presidential decree annulling

republican laws which allowed young men to avoid being conscripted into the Soviet Army.

The biggest bombshell of all came on 20 December. Foreign Minister Eduard Shevardnadze, a man hated by the hardliners, because they blamed him as much as Gorbachev for giving up the second empire, stood up in the Supreme Soviet to deliver 'the shortest and most difficult speech of my life.' Warning that dictatorship was coming, Shevardnadze announced his resignation. The shock-waves were felt across the world. This was a man whom the West had come to trust and believe, one who was not given to empty gestures. The world joined the Soviet people in watching and waiting with bated breath as to what 1991 would bring.

12
FROM CRACKDOWN TO COLLAPSE

The world did not have long to wait before Eduard Shevardnadze's words began to come true. In the New Year, the Kremlin began to turn the screw on the Baltic states: on 2 January, troops from the Soviet Interior Ministry seized a printing house in the Latvian capital, Riga; later that week, in line with President Gorbachev's December decree on conscription, Soviet Army troops began scouring the three republics for young men who had avoided military service.

The signs grew worse. On 10 January, Gorbachev sent an ultimatum to the Lithuanian parliament in which he accused its members of 'gross breaches of the Constitution of the USSR.' Six months earlier, the Lithuanians would no doubt have been delighted to reply, affirming that they had indeed acted in this way, but reminding the Soviet president that, as far as they were concerned, they were no longer a part of the Soviet Union, and thus not governed by the Soviet Constitution. By now the tension was increasing by the hour, and the time for such bravado was past. The next day, a shadowy 'National Salvation Committee' was formed in Lithuania. One of its first demands was the imposition of presidential rule from Moscow. On the same day, the 11th, Soviet soldiers seized the main press building in Vilnius, the Lithuanian capital.

The storm clouds finally broke on 13 January. Soviet Army troops in tanks and armored personnel carriers stormed the television tower in Vilnius. The soldiers easily swept through the crowds of unarmed people surrounding the building. In any case, as in Baku 12 months earlier and Tbilisi in April 1989, the troops had orders not to stand on ceremony. Thirteen people died, some shot, others crushed beneath the tracks of the tanks.

This time, however, there was not just one short sharp lesson. The Balts had feared – particularly after Shevardnadze's resignation – that the Kremlin would take advantage of the world's attention being distracted by the crisis in the Gulf, where the Allied powers' ultimatum to the Iraqi leader Saddam Hussein to pull out of Kuwait was fast running out. Moscow had used this tactic before, invading Hungary in 1956 while the West was preoccupied with the Suez Crisis. History was, to a degree, repeating itself.

The Allies' ultimatum to Saddam – withdraw from Kuwait or face armed intervention – expired on 15 January, two days after the killings in Vilnius. In the early hours of the 17th, the first air-

BELOW: 9 January 1991, Lithuanians in Vilnius respond to a call to defend their parliament as the threat of action by the Soviet Army grows.

craft bombed Baghdad. The Soviet Union was supporting the Allies morally, though not with troops on the ground. As it was, Gorbachev very nearly wrecked the Allies' element of surprise. A few hours before the assault started he was made privy to the decision to begin the liberation of Kuwait. In a final attempt to be seen as the mediator, the Soviet president tried to contact Saddam to tell him to withdraw his forces, but no link-up could be made between Moscow and Baghdad.

Telephone communications had also proved poor back home. When the storming of the television tower began on 13 January, Lithuanian President Vytautas Landsbergis tried to call Gorbachev, but was unable to raise him. Gorbachev was later to deny all prior knowledge of the Army's action in Vilnius, as were Defense Minister Marshal Dmitry Yazov and Boris Pugo, whose Interior Ministry troops were also involved. If these three men really did know nothing about plans for military action, then the Army was beginning to act as a law unto itself. It was just conceivable, though, that Gorbachev, Yazov and Pugo might not have been telling the whole truth.

Tension mounted in Riga, too. On the 16th, one man was shot, allegedly for not stopping at a checkpoint which had no right to be there in the first place. Four days later, a unit of the by now notorious Interior Ministry riot squads, the OMON, attacked the Latvian Interior Ministry. Five people died. If what was happening bore a frightening resemblance to past Soviet actions, there were also signs of fresh hope. In 1956 there had been no-one within the Soviet Union – or the

Warsaw Pact – ready to raise their voice in the Hungarians' defense. But in January 1991, Russia had its own non-Communist leader who was not afraid of angering the Soviet establishment. Boris Yeltsin flew to Estonia, where he met the three Baltic presidents and signed a joint declaration condemning the use of force in the Baltic States. He angered Gorbachev further by suggesting publicly that Russian soldiers serving in

ABOVE: Vytautas Landsbergis, leader of the independence movement, Sajudis, and the first post-Communist President of Lithuania. His dictatorial style was to see him voted out of office before the end of 1992.

LEFT: On 13 January, the moment the Balts had feared arrived. Soviet troops forcibly took the television tower in Vilnius, killing 13 unarmed civilians in the process. The troops remained in occupation of the TV tower until after the failed coup in August.

RIGHT: Boris Yeltsin meets representatives of the Ingush people, March 1991, whilst on a tour of the Northern Caucasus. This region, with its many tribes, was to prove a headache for the Russian leader both before and since the break-up of the Soviet Union.

the region should question any future orders of that nature.

Yeltsin was not alone. A week after the violence in Vilnius (and just hours before the five deaths in Riga), 250,000 Muscovites demonstrated against the use of force in the Baltic states. True, the vast majority of the capital's residents did something else that Sunday afternoon; but such a show of solidarity illustrated to the Balts that they did not stand alone.

The Soviet leadership, though, was becoming more hardline, both in personalities and policies.

In December, Gorbachev had pushed the appointment of Gennedy Yanaev as vice-president through the Supreme Soviet. A grey figure, Yanaev was a classic Communist *apparatchik* to whom the word 'reform' was anathema. Yanaev's appointment was followed by that of another man from the same mold, Valentin Pavlov, who took over as prime minister on 14 January.

One of Pavlov's first actions was to announce that 50 and 100 rouble notes were being withdrawn from circulation, and that people could

RIGHT: A pro-Yeltsin rally on Moscow's Manege Square two days before the elections for the first Russian President on 12 June 1991. Such rallies were very much a feature of political life in the last three years of Soviet power, but the harsh economic realities which followed saw a marked decline in political interest.

exchange a maximum of 1000 roubles. The reason cited – that unnamed Western banks were planning an economic coup in the USSR – was so ludicrous that it was soon quietly dropped, but this kind of rhetoric was becoming all too common from the entourage with which Gorbachev was surrounding himself.

On 17 March Gorbachev was able to pretend that he had the backing of the people for a renewed Soviet Union. A nationwide referendum took place on the future of the country. The question asked of the electorate was: 'Do you consider it necessary to preserve the Union of Soviet Socialist Republics as a renewed federation of equal sovereign republics, in which human rights and the freedom of all nationalities will be fully guaranteed?'

Two-thirds of those taking part voted in favor, but Gorbachev's claim that this showed that he was on the right track was a hollow one. The three Baltic states did not take part, but held their own polls on independence. The massive votes in favor were dismissed by the Soviet president as 'illegal,' Georgia, Moldova and Armenia also refused to hold the referendum. Indeed, the way in which the question on the referendum was worded made it difficult to vote 'no.' After all, if you did, you could be accused of voting against human rights, or against freedom for all the nationalities of the USSR.

A more significant demonstration of the public mood came on 28 March. Hardliners in the Russian parliament were planning a vote of no-confidence in their chairman, Boris Yeltsin. A massive public show of support for Yeltsin was arranged in Moscow for the eve of the session. The Soviet authorities banned the demonstration, but the Moscow city authorities gave permission for it to go ahead. This illustrated the growing anarchy within society and it also seemed to set the scene for a showdown between the reformers and the hardliners.

Thanks to a late agreement made behind the scenes, the demonstration passed off peacefully. What was more, the next day Yeltsin won the support of parliament, not only to defeat the no-confidence motion, but to increase his powers. It was also agreed that Russia would have its own president, the election to take place on 12 June.

Before the election, there was one final sign that Gorbachev and Yeltsin might still be able to work together. Pressing ahead with his plan for a renewed Soviet Union, Gorbachev succeeded in getting the leaders of nine republics – including Russia – to sign an agreement to this effect in April. Gorbachev was not to know that the '9 + 1 Agreement' as it was known – Gorbachev being the 'one' – was to trigger off the attempted seizure of power by the hardliners. The final treaty was to be signed on 20 August. If the hardliners were to make a move, it would have to be before this date.

When the Russian presidential election took place, Boris Yeltsin romped home as the clear winner, with well over the statutory 50 percent of the vote in the first round. Of the other five candidates, the heavy defeat of former Soviet Prime Minister Nikolai Ryzhkov showed the increasing polarization of politics in the country. Ryzhkov and others like him had not embraced the outspoken reformism of Yeltsin, but they were also well removed from the backward-looking philosophy prevalent among those surrounding Gorbachev.

Hindsight is a wonderful thing. With the benefit of it, it is now possible to see two crucial pointers as to what was to happen in Moscow on 19 August which, had they been heeded, might have led to very different results. Early in August, Eduard Shevardnadze resigned from the Communist Party. Shortly after this, on the 12th, he warned that 'destructive forces are gaining momentum' in society. Four days later, Aleksandr Yakovlev, formerly Gorbachev's right-hand man, declared that 'a party and state coup' was in the offing.

Since the beginning of August, President Gorbachev had been on holiday at his sumptuous

ABOVE: Boris Yeltsin about to cast his vote in the presidential election, June 1991. Despite there being six candidates, Yeltsin comfortably passed the 50 percent plus one requirement in the first ballot.

RIGHT: The failed coup, 19 August 1991. Demonstrators surround Soviet Army vehicles in the center of Moscow, whilst a young woman climbs on board an armored personnel carrier to remonstrate with the commander.

BELOW: Day two of the coup. President Yeltsin with armed bodyguard in the Russian parliament building, known as 'the White House.' This became the symbol of resistance to the coup. There were strong fears that it would be stormed on the night of 20-21 August, but in the end the Emergency Committee lost their nerve.

dacha at Foros in the Crimea. He was due to return to Moscow on 19 August, a Monday, ready to sign the new union treaty the next day. On the Sunday afternoon, a delegation arrived unexpectedly at the dacha. They said that they were from the State Committee for the State of Emergency, and demanded Gorbachev's resignation. Gorbachev, as he later admitted, told them in the most basic terms to return from whence they came. This they did, but the president and his entourage were now prisoners in the presidential dacha.

For Muscovites and the rest of the world, the coup began at 6.00am on Monday 19 August 1991. This was when Radio Moscow broadcast the announcement that, owing to illness, President Gorbachev had relinquished his duties, and a state of emergency was now in force. Just as in times of national mourning – such as when the head of state had died – the radio began playing solemn music. The announcement was just about the only aspect of the coup which the Emergency Committee got right. In just about every other respect, the events of 19 to 21 August were a perfect example of how not to organize the overthrow of a state. Perhaps the plotters assumed that people were so fed up with affairs in the country that they would be bound to support them. It certainly seems that they ignored the crucial change which Gorbachev's rule had brought to Russia: people in general were no longer afraid of the authorities as they had been in the old days.

One of the plotters' main errors would appear to have been the failure to recognize the importance of Russian – as opposed to Soviet – institutions. Boris Yeltsin had become so important to Russia that it seems incredible to think that the coup leaders did not think to arrest him until after the coup had been declared. By this time, he had already held a council of war at his dacha outside Moscow and departed for the Russian parliament building, the White House.

When the first tanks pulled up outside parliament, Yeltsin established his authority by going out of the building to the first one, shaking hands with its bewildered crew members, and then standing on its decks and publicly denouncing the coup. Although at that time very few people had gathered around the White House, news of the Russian President's defiant action quickly spread (another failure of the plotters was not to cut telephone lines or prevent radio stations from broadcasting). The White House became the symbol of resistance to the coup. By Monday evening, thousands of people surrounded it, many of them staying there all night to defy the curfew imposed by the Emergency Committee. Ten of the tanks which had been sent against the parliament turned their guns around to show they were now defending it.

Twenty-four hours after it began, it was already evident that support for the coup throughout the country was at best lukewarm. Though it had been welcomed by many old-style Communists who were still in charge of their little domains the length and breadth of Russia,

LEFT: A demonstrator waves the flag of the Republican Party of Russia as crowds watch and wait outside the White House, 20 August.

BELOW: Many of the soldiers sent in by the Emergency Committee were confused by what they were being asked to do. Others, including 10 tanks outside the White House, turned their guns around to show that they were prepared to defend the Russian parliament, not the Emergency Committee.

the coup faced serious problems. The personal authority of Leningrad's mayor, Anatoly Sobchak, had ensured that it was already on the

RIGHT: First doubts about the viability of the coup came when members of the Emergency Committee gave a Press conference on the afternoon of the 19th. (l to r) Interior Minister Boris Pugo, Vice-President Gennady Yanaev and Oleg Baklanov. Yanaev's hands shook throughout the Press conference, and his speech was slurred, leading to the general conclusion that he was drunk. The day after the coup failed, Pugo shot himself and his wife.

brink of collapse there; miners had gone on strike in protest at the coup in the Siberian Kuzbass fields, in Ukraine and Belorussia; and the one time that the coup leaders had appeared to try and convince people that all was well – at a Press conference on the Monday afternoon – they had looked ill-at-ease and decidedly unconvincing.

On Tuesday evening, the showdown came. There was the first violence of the coup. A column of armored personnel carriers was moving through the center of Moscow, but found it blocked by barricades. The troops were surrounded by protesters and panicked. In frantically trying to extricate himself from the crowds, one driver caught one of the protesters in the tracks of his vehicle and the man was torn to shreds.

Angry crowds stormed the vehicles, the troops opened fire and a second man died. As the troops tried to escape, a third victim was run

BELOW: Makeshift barricades block approaches to the White House, 19 August.

over. The spot where the deaths occurred – the underpass on the Garden Ring Road where it is crossed by Kalinin Prospect (now renamed Novy Arbat) – became a shrine to the three men. As well as the spontaneous gestures by Muscovites of placing flowers and candles on the spot, in the aftermath of the coup the Moscow authorities laid a patch of red asphalt on the road. Some 400m away, at the White House itself, the atmosphere was tense. Rumors abounded that the Army was preparing to attack the building. Had it done so, there can be little doubt that what had been until now a clumsy and bungled attempt to seize power would have turned into widespread civil war.

A significant number of people had shown themselves to be, if not actively in favor, then not actually against the coup, yet thousands of others had shown they were prepared to die rather than give up their recently acquired freedom. More importantly, the Army was divided in its support, which would have meant that both sides possessed powerful weaponry. In such circumstances, it would have been very difficult to stop the momentum toward violence which an attack on the White House would have provoked.

But no attack came. The coup leaders realized that they had blown their chance, and decided against making their final act an apocalyptic one. The next morning, Wednesday 21 August, Yeltsin declared to the Russian parliament that 'a group of tourists' – three of the plotters with their entourage – had been seen heading for Moscow's Vnukovo Airport. The coup was degenerating into farce. Russian deputies voted to send a delegation after them. Yeltsin, however, was not allowed to go in case it was a trap. More appropriately, the senior figure was retired air force colonel and Afghan War hero Vice-President Aleksandr Rutskoi.

The Russian delegation arrived at the airport an hour after the coup leaders' aircraft had taken off for the Crimea. They followed. The absurd chase ended at Foros in Gorbachev's dacha. The Soviet president refused to see Defense Minister Yazov or the head of the KGB, Kryuchkov. The only member of the first delegation that he agreed to see was his old friend Anatoly Lukyanov, who did his best to distance himself from the coup. It was a sign of just how out of touch Gorbachev was – despite later paying thanks to the BBC and other foreign broadcasters for keeping him informed of what was going on in Moscow – that he was prepared to believe Lukyanov.

The mopping-up of the coup was swift. On the Wednesday afternoon, the tanks returned to their barracks. All of the coup leaders were arrested, except for Interior Minister Boris Pugo, who shot himself. Having returned to Moscow in the early hours of Thursday morning, Gorbachev gave a Press conference that afternoon, but it was an embarrassing affair which underlined that, as the coup leaders had wanted, he was on the way out. Instead of denouncing the Communist Party, Gorbachev made the mistake of continuing to profess his belief in its ideas.

LEFT: A tired-looking Mikhail Gorbachev returns to Moscow in the early hours of 22 August. Despite having followed events thanks to the BBC World Service and other foreign stations, Gorbachev was to prove out of touch with the changes of mood that had taken place in his absence. Though it failed, the coup was the beginning of the end for Gorbachev and the Soviet Union.

RIGHT: President Yeltsin waves a Russian flag during the rally on 22 August to celebrate the defeat of the coup.

RIGHT: President Yeltsin waves a Russian flag during the rally on 22 August to celebrate the defeat of the coup.

There was more in the same vein the next day, when Gorbachev appeared before the Russian parliament. When Boris Yeltsin forced him publicly to read out the list of those implicated in the coup, Gorbachev was forced to admit that the whole Soviet government should resign. It was the next day, Saturday, that Gorbachev resigned as party General Secretary, by which time the Moscow city authorities had already begun seizing the party's property in the capital.

Although the Soviet Union continued in name for another four months, it effectively died with the coup. The pseudo-independence of the Baltic states immediately became reality, with international recognition of the three countries in early September. On 5 September, the Soviet

Congress of People's Deputies voted itself out of existence. Yet Gorbachev – and, it should be said, many others – still refused to believe that the Soviet republics could exist independently of each other. On 18 October, Gorbachev persuaded eight of the nine republican leaders who had signed the agreement for the new union treaty in April – Ukraine refused to take part – to sign a new document, laying the ground for the Union of Sovereign States (USS). This envisaged a zone of economic cooperation on the territory of the former USSR, but without some form of political cooperation, such an agreement was meaningless.

Just how meaningless was shown on 1 December, when the people of Ukraine voted overwhelmingly in a referendum to support their government's declaration of independence. Dismissing the vote, Gorbachev stated – rightly – that there could be no union without Ukraine, and – wrongly – that there could be no Ukraine without the union. Of all the former Soviet republics, Ukraine looked the most viable as an independent state. Territorially about the size of France, and with a population slightly smaller than that of Britain, there were plenty of examples that could be cited as to why Ukraine – rich in arable land and natural resources – should survive the break-up of the union better than most.

The Ukrainian vote seemed to be the signal that Boris Yeltsin had been waiting for. Although a signatory to the USS agreement, it seems certain that the Russian president was simply marking time until he could be sure of support for his own plan. A week after the Ukrainian poll, Yeltsin met with Leonid Kravchuk, the Ukrainian president, and Belorussian leader Stanislav Shushkevich and, after a day's talks, signed an agreement on 8 December which stated that the Soviet Union no longer existed and that they were forming the Commonwealth of Independent States (CIS).

This was the real coup of 1991. Gorbachev had been completely outflanked by the three Slav republics. Without Russia and Ukraine, no other union could possibly be at all effective in the post-Soviet era. The non-Slav republics protested at their apparent exclusion from the new agreement. However, a meeting was arranged for 21 December in the Kazakh capital, Alma-Ata, at which all 12 of the post-August coup Soviet states were invited to sign up for the CIS. The Slav republics agreed that this would be taken as the founding date of the Commonwealth, thus apparently not giving them any unfair advantage. Of the 12, only Georgia, struggling with its own civil war, refused to join.

Gorbachev had been presented with a *fait accompli*. He and his union had been rejected by all those who were supposed to be its members. It had also been emphasized to him that he had no role to play in the new organization; he had not even been invited to Alma-Ata. Gorbachev held a nine-hour meeting with Boris Yeltsin on 25 December 1991. By now, it was not a conversation between a tenant and his landlord; Yeltsin had bought the house and Gorbachev was handing over the keys. At 7 o'clock that evening, Gorbachev made a brief appearance on television to bid farewell to the people he no longer ruled. Twenty minutes after he finished, the Soviet flag over the Kremlin was run down, and replaced with the Russian white, blue and red tricolor. The Soviet Union – and the Soviet empire – was no more.

LEFT: Muscovites celebrate the coup's collapse, 22 August.

13
THOUGHTS ON THE FUTURE

LEFT: Lithuania proclaimed independence in
March 1990. It became an internationally-
recognized fact in August 1991.

The collapse of the Soviet empire caused more new problems than it solved old ones. Many of these are due to the way in which the economy was run. In a deliberate attempt to make the republics dependent on each other, and thus try to ensure the survival of the Union, no republic, not even Russia, was self-sufficient, especially in light industry. For example, the only plant in the whole of the USSR which made electricity meters was in Lithuania; the only factory making male contraceptives was in Azerbaijan.

Defense was another area left in a mess by the collapse of the Union. The defense of the Soviet Union was organized not according to republican boundaries, but by military districts (MDs), which in turn formed theaters of military operations (TVDs). The borders of both MDs and TVDs transgressed republican borders. When newly-independent republics declared that they were forming their own armies, they took over military equipment on their territory. This gave the new Ukrainian army, for instance, a vast preponderance of tanks, since the south western TVD into which it fell was regarded as particularly important to defend against possible attack through Central or Southern Europe.

Taking over military equipment that happened to be on a republic's territory also gave rise to the dispute between Russia and Ukraine over who owned the Black Sea Fleet. Ukraine claimed it did, because it was based in Ukraine; Russia denounced this as nonsense, saying that the fleet had always been Russian. In the summer of 1992, a shaky compromise was reached, whereby the two republics agreed to joint control over the fleet.

Nuclear weapons were another issue which divided republics. The Soviet nuclear arsenal was based in Russia, Ukraine, Belorussia and Kazakhstan. The worry for the world was, did this mean that suddenly there were four nuclear powers where previously one had existed? The presidents of Ukraine, Belorussia and Kazakhstan eventually agreed to send all tactical nuclear weapons back to Russia, a task which was completed by the end of May 1992. But while Belorussia and Kazakhstan readily agreed to get rid of their strategic missiles, Kiev was less enthusiastic, and pressure remained in parliament to hang on to them, as a bargaining chip both with Russia and the outside world.

If nuclear weapons were a macro post-Soviet problem, there was a highly significant micro problem, which would also not be solved overnight. This was the question of *Homo sovieticus*, or the new Soviet man. The *Homo sovieticus* theory grew up in the 1920s. Communist scientists believed that the theory of Marxism-Leni-

RIGHT: A Russian sailor arm-wrestles with a Ukrainian sailor in a bout of friendly rivalry amongst servicemen of the Black Sea Fleet. The wrangles between Russia and Ukraine over the future ownership of the Fleet (below left) were less amicable until Presidents Yeltsin and Kravchuk agreed a compromise in summer 1992.

BELOW: The new political geography of Eastern Europe and the Russian Federation.

nism was so different from anything that had preceded it, that it would be possible to produce a new being, the Soviet man. Soviet man would be exempt from the nastier characteristics of mankind, and would be a caring creature, living in a new, caring society.

In actual fact, the Soviet system did succeed in producing its own type of man; but it was not the *Homo sovieticus* which the scientists had had in mind. Thanks to the one-party political system, the new Soviet man learned not to tolerate any opinions which contradicted his own. The failure of the system to deliver made him adept at spouting wonderful words about the future, none of which had any hope of being fulfilled. Because of the shortcomings of the system, he learned quickly that the best way to get on in life was by a combination of cheating, bribing and deceit.

It was against this background, then, that the former Soviet republics were set the task of establishing their independence. The first to break free, the Baltic states of Estonia, Latvia and Lithuania, reveled in their re-found political freedom; they were also in the forefront of moves to introduce their own currencies, thus cutting that last economic tie with the former Soviet Union.

It soon became clear that independence would not shake off the Soviet legacy of a moribund economic system which guaranteed its people a low standard of living. Nor have their leaders escaped behaving in the bombastic manner of *Homo sovieticus*. Nevertheless, a Western desire to make up for 50 years when in theory they maintained that the three republics were not a part of the USSR, but in practice regarded them as such, means that the Baltic states stand a good chance of surviving and prospering in the years to come.

Belorussia and Ukraine have used their geographical closeness to Western Europe to begin establishing links with the European Community and individual West European countries. Both republics were hampered on the road to establishing new, democratic systems by the preponderance of old-style Communists in their post-Soviet leaderships. In Ukraine in particular, the former party *apparatchik* Leonid Kravchuk took advantage of splits in the nationalist movement, Rukh, to take firm control after his election as president in December 1991. The repression by force of anti-government protesters in September 1992 did not bode well for the swift establishment of democracy in Ukraine.

Problems of economic independence were emphasized when Ukraine brought in coupons to replace roubles early in 1992, as a forerunner to the introduction of their own currency, the hrivna. As the proposed date for the hrivna's arrival slipped from summer 1992 back into 1993, so the value of the coupon fell even lower than

that of Russia's rouble, already regarded by many as virtually worthless.

Moldova's independence was marred from the start by the problem created by Stalin after he incorporated Moldova into the Union. Stalin added the Trans-Dniester region – never a part of Moldova – to the republic. When many Moldovans spoke of reunification with Rumania, the Trans-Dniestrians – largely Russians and Ukrainians – brought about a virtual civil war in the region. There is no easy solution which will please all sides.

Civil war was the fate of the Transcaucasian republics, too. Trouble flared in Georgia in September 1991, as opposition grew to the ever-more dictatorial methods adopted by the elected president, Zviad Gamsakhurdia. A former dissident, who had been imprisoned for speaking out against the Soviet regime, Gamsakhurdia used classic Communist methods to deal with his opponents. His ousting from power in January 1992, and the return to Georgia of the former Soviet Foreign Minister Eduard Shevardnadze two months later brought only a temporary calm.

If it is difficult to see a swift end to civil strife in Georgia, then farther south, in the conflict between Armenia and Azerbaijan, it looks impossible. This is the longest-running ethnic dispute in the former Soviet Union, trouble having first flared in February 1988 after Armenian demands for the return of the enclave of Nagorny Karabakh. Since then, thousands have died, both in Karabakh itself and as the conflict has spilled over into nearby Azeri and Armenian territory. International peace talks in 1992 failed to achieve a breakthrough, and, with the two sides main-

ABOVE: Tactical nuclear weapons being dismantled in Ukraine before being sent back to Russia to be destroyed. All tactical nuclear weapons were back in Russia by May 1992.

RIGHT: No end in sight in Karabakh. Far from leading to an end to hostilities, the break-up of the Soviet Union was followed by an intensification of the fighting between Armenia and Karabakh. This skirmish, in Azerbaijan, outside Karabakh, was typical of the spread of the fighting towards the end of 1992.

taining totally intransigent positions, prospects for peace in the medium term look distinctly remote.

The Central Asian republics – Kazakhstan, Kyrgyzstan, Tajikistan, Turkmenistan and Uzbekistan – have also not moved totally peacefully into the post-Soviet era. In many ways, this region had gained the most from Soviet rule, given how backward it was before the revolution. Their fear at the thought of being left to fend for themselves was evident when they pro-

tested loudly at the signing by Russia, Ukraine and Belorussia of the initial agreement for the Commonwealth of Independent States. Their relief was evident when they were invited to become signatories two weeks later.

The worst trouble in the months following the collapse of the Soviet Union came in Tajikistan, where President Rakhmon Nabiyev – another former Communist *apparatchik* – was finally ousted following near-civil war in the country. But even after Nabiyev was thrown out trouble

continued. There were stirrings of unrest in other Central Asian republics, notably Uzbekistan, which suggest that the road to democracy and peace will be a long and bumpy one in this part of the former Soviet Union.

Although these former parts of the Soviet empire are struggling with the problems brought by independence, at the heart of the former country an empire still remains: that of Russia. Even after the break-up of the Soviet Union, Russia remains the biggest (geographically) country in the world. But its 150 million inhabitants come from over 100 different nationalities, and even before the collapse of the USSR, some of these nationalities were calling for independence from Russia.

The Soviet system granted a measure of recognition to some of the nationalities, by forming autonomous regions (*oblasti*) and autonomous republics, based on the main national group in the area, but in practice, these were merely administrative divisions. There may have been a cursory bow to local culture and traditions, such as allowing schools to teach local, as well as Soviet, history, but the title 'autonomous' did not imply any real political or economic freedom.

Thanks to Mikhail Gorbachev's policy of *glasnost*, nationalities within the Russian federation began to find their voices. One of the first was the Tatars. Their homeland, Tatarstan, lies some

800kms east of Moscow, about half way to the Ural Mountains which divide European Russia from Asian Russia. A long-standing, though long-silenced, grudge which the Tatars held against Moscow was that 98 percent of the revenue earned by Tatarstan's industry and the exploitation of its natural resources went to the all-Union budget.

Calls for Tatar independence grew throughout 1990, and reached a notable peak in June 1991 when Tatarstan did not take part in the election of the Russian president. Instead, Tatarstan elected its own president, Mintimer Shaimiev. Another Communist *apparatchik*, Shaimiev did at least succeed in keeping in check the more extreme nationalist elements. This was vital, since only about half of Tatarstan's four million population are actually Tatars, the overwhelming majority of the others being Russians. A further six million Tatars live in other parts of the former Soviet Union. If ethnic strife erupted in Tatarstan it would have far-reaching consequences.

Far more militant than Shaimiev is Dzhokar Dudaev, president of the would-be breakaway republic of Chechnya. Formerly called Chechen-Ingushetia, Chechnya is a small region in the Northern Caucasus, which proclaimed its independence from Russia in November 1991. Following armed clashes, President Yeltsin sent troops to the capital, Grozny, but short of

BELOW: January 1992. A demonstration in Senaki, western Georgia, in support of the ousted Georgian President Zviad Gamsakhurdia. Georgia collapsed into civil war soon after the failed coup. The opposition to Gamsakhurdia accused him of using dictatorial methods to rule. Even the return to Georgia of former Soviet Foreign Minister Eduard Shevardnadze in March 1992, and his election as President the following October, did not bring an end to the troubles.

LEFT: The face of Russia, 1992. The Russian government's economic shock therapy in freeing prices brought further chaos and pushed as many as 90 percent of the population below the poverty line.

causing a bloodbath, there was nothing the troops could do. They remained at the airport before being withdrawn a few days later.

The Grozny episode illustrated Moscow's impotence in dealing with such events. If the Russian government resorts to using force, then

RIGHT: Fierce fighting took place in Moldova in 1992, between the local population and ethnic Russians and Ukrainians living in the Trans-Dniester region. In the city of Bendery in June things became so bad that not even the corpses could be removed.

it faces the accusation that it is trying to preserve the empire against the wishes of the people. On the other hand, it will come under strong pressure from its own people, and especially outspoken Russian nationalists, to protect the interests of Russians, wherever they may be.

Throughout 1992 there were ominous sounds emanating from Moscow about sending troops to areas such as Trans-Dniester to protect Russians there. If there is sustained violence against Russians in the Russian Federation itself, there seems little doubt that pressure to

RIGHT: April 1992. A pro-Communist demonstrator holding a caricature of Yeltsin as a butcher, preparing to sell off slices of Russia to Westerners. Popular support for the hardliners grew in 1992 as life became tougher.

use force will grow, possibly to the point where it is overwhelming.

It is difficult to see a bright future for Russia, certainly in the short term. With the economy in chaos and nationalism growing even among the smallest of ethnic groups, the potential is there for the Russian Federation – the Russian empire – to tear itself apart.

In the latter years of Soviet power, many Russians compared the mood in the country with the uncertainty of the period between the March and November Revolutions of 1917. In the post-Soviet period, a more accurate comparison is with Germany in the 1920s: hyper-inflation, political instability, and a proud nation which has been humiliated by a cataclysm – for Germany, World War I; for Russia, the collapse of Communism. Just as in Germany a dictator rose from the ashes to impose order on chaos, there is a strong possibility that this could be Russia's fate. The Soviet empire may have fallen, but the reverberations will be felt for many years.

ABOVE: Lenin could be waving goodbye, as his statue is removed from Riga, Latvia, in August 1991. The Soviet Union's legacy is chaos, hardship and continuing ethnic and civil unrest.

INDEX

ACKNOWLEDGMENTS

The author and publisher would like to thank Martin Bristow for designing this book, Sara Dunphy and Stephen Small for the picture research, Richard Natkiel for the maps and Ron Watson for the index. The following individuals and agencies provided photographs:

The Bettmann Archive, pages: 9, 10(both), 12, 14(top), 16(top), 17(both), 19(bottom), 22-23, 24(both), 31(bottom), 33(bottom), 34(bottom), 35(both), 36(top), 43(top), 51(top), 101.
Brompton Books, page: 38.
David King Collection, pages: 18(top), 20, 21(bottom), 25(bottom), 28, 30(both), 31(top), 32(bottom), 47(bottom).
Life File, pages: 2-3(Mike Potter), 6(Oleg Svyatoslavsky).
Novosti Press Agency, pages: 8, 14(bottom), 15(top), 16(bottom), 19(top), 21(top), 29(bottom), 37, 60, 99(bottom).
Reuters/Bettmann Newsphotos, pages: 64(top), 79(bottom), 80(both), 81(both), 85(top), 92, 94, 98, 102(bottom), 103(both), 104, 105(both), 107(top), 108, 110, 111, 113(both), 114, 115(both), 116, 117, 118(both), 119(both), 120(both), 121, 122, 124, 125(both), 126(both), 127, 128, 129, 130(both), 131(both), 132, 134(both), 135, 136, 138, 139(both), 140(both), 141, 142(both), 143(both), 144(top), 145, 147, 148, 150, 151, 152(top), 154, 155, 156(bottom), 157.
TASS, pages: 50, 70, 99(top), 100, 133, 144(bottom), 146, 152(bottom), 153(both), 156(top).
UPI/Bettmann Newsphotos, pages: 11, 18(bottom), 25(top), 26, 29(top), 32(top), 33(top), 34(top), 36(bottom), 40, 41(both), 42(both), 43(bottom), 44(both), 45, 46, 47(top), 48, 51, 52(both), 53(both), 54(both), 55, 56(both), 57(both), 58(both), 59, 60, 63(both), 64(bottom), 65, 66(both), 67, 68(both), 69, 71(both), 72, 73, 74, 76, 77(both), 78, 79(top), 82, 83, 84(both), 85(bottom), 86, 88, 89, 90, 91(both), 93, 95, 96, 102(top), 106, 107(bottom), 112.